Y0-EFZ-366

PRIMER
FOR THE
BEGINNING
TEACHER

Francis A. Filardo
Master Teacher, 41 Years

Prior Press of Lakewood, Inc.
P.O. Box 546, Lakewood, N.J. 08701

PRIMER FOR THE
BEGINNING TEACHER

Copyright 1998

All rights reserved. No part of this book may be reproduced in any form except for the inclusion of brief quotations in a review or article without permission from the author or publisher.

Published by:

**PRIOR PRESS OF LAKEWOOD
P.O. BOX 546
LAKEWOOD, N.J. 08701**

Printed by:

**MORRIS PRINTING
3212 East Highway 30
Kearney, NE. 68847**

ISBN: 0-7392-0026-7

Library of Congress Catalog Card Number: 98-94900

This book is dedicated to my best friend, my greatest blessing, my precious wife, Emilia.

"It's never raining when I'm with you, my love."

FOREWORD

Primer for the Beginning Teacher was written to aid the fledging who is set to enter the unknown downward drafts of a hopefully long career in education. The shock of reality will quickly replace the collegiate dream fantasies of "Goodbye Mr. Chips" mentality. The golden brick road painted by most theoretical college professors yesterday has many potholes. More than a few teachers have been terminated in these canyons of unexpected obstacles.

The book assists the beginner and was formatted as a monthly guide at the start of a school year. In retrospect, forty-one years of actual experience spanning grades five through twelve, hasn't removed the apprehensiveness once felt on my first day of teaching an equally anxious class of twenty-five neatly scrubbed fifth graders. That first day found me standing in front of my class wondering just where to begin. Fortunately, my colleague in the next classroom suggested I should have the class recite the pledge of allegiance.

With a blissful naïve beginning, little did I know of the serious demands professional relationships with my colleagues, administrators, trustees, janitors, secretaries, aides, parents, and a handful of emotionally disturbed children.

How will the beginning teacher deal with a class of twenty-five children, each having different learning capabilities in every subject? How will the novice deal with an administrator's criticism? What will be your answer when asked by a parent, "What is your educational philosophy?" It has been reported that the average employment expectancy of a superintendent is less than four years. This writer has had thirty-six different administrators during the forty-one years of teaching. This number includes sixteen superintendents coupled with principals.

The new teacher should be flexible enough to teach in an environment whose spectrum ranges from the ultra-liberal, free-wheeling philosophy of "less is more?" This ridiculous concept promotes less time teaching children in the classroom and advocates more children time with nonsensical frivolities. Conversely, the ultra-conservative right winger promotes an equally perverse and myopic dunderhead programs of banning books and promoting self-designed personal agendas.

Primer for the Beginning Teacher is not a panacea for all problems in every school district. It is an informative work that was written to assist the

novice achieve a long and extremely rewarding
lifelong experience.

Francis A. Filardo
December, 1998

CONTENTS

SEPTEMBER

The Beginning

After a summer of fun or frustration, the school year begins with a teacher orientation. All teachers of most school systems usually gather in a large room or auditorium with the principal, superintendent and members of the board of education. The superintendent reviews highlights of the past year and expectations for the new one. A board of education trustee usually greets the staff with some gracious comments. Finally, the local teacher association distributes copies of the new teacher contractual agreement and/or relays pertinent information.

At noon, teachers are sometimes treated to a lunch before either dispersing for localized meetings or preparing the classrooms for the next day's opening. Old Glory is placed in the classroom flag holder followed by decorating the walls with pictures pertaining to subject matter as well as adding a little aesthetic beauty.

Some teachers pile different subject books in the front of the classroom for the next day's distribution while others prefer to have the first student in each row go to the closet or filing cabinet for the amount of books needed.

After book distribution, the teacher records the book number of each child's book. This is necessary when books are returned in June. Lost or destroyed books must be paid for before the issuance of the final report card. Student hall lockers and combination locks are then distributed, assigned, and recorded either on index cards or in a teacher's notebook.

NUTS AND BOLTS

With the frenzied activities of a new school year, many teachers overlook reviewing the permanent record and experience folder of each assigned child in their classes. It is an extremely useful practice to peruse any and all pertinent remarks found within folder. In addition to telephone numbers, intelligence quotient, and California Test of Basic Skills (C.T.B.S.) scores noting str engths and weaknesses in various subjects, comments from previous teachers should be read. This is not to pre-judge but to be made aware of any physical, social, emotional, or mental problems. Nurse's comments as to allergies or aliments are also extremely important. The Child Study Team comments should also be noted. This is important because some children may have a severe emotional problem. A parent may have recently died or perhaps were divorced. I remember reading about a father being unemployed because of the closing of a plant. He pulled hair out of his wife's head and told his children, "We don't have any food because you kids eat too much!" My interaction with that particular student took on a different dimension. Another father told me of his wife leaving him to live with another woman in Greenwich Village. He has two daughters.

SEATING

Classroom seating arrangements vary with almost every teacher. Some like to have children sit in a circle, covered wagon style. Others prefer groups sitting together in twos, fours, or six clusters. Most have children sitting in six or seven rows, one desk behind another. I have tried almost all techniques, and I'm sure you will. What I continually revert back to is having one desk behind the other in rows of six or seven. It is easier for me to keep track of children I ask questions of and it reduces distractions. This teacher's usual teaching technique is called the "Socratic Method." I seldom give answers to any question asked. I keep asking a student questions until that student gives birth to knowledge and answers the question asked. There are many teaching techniques. Find a technique that suits your style and is successful.

When children are seated alphabetically it facilitates distributing thousands of test papers, office notices that have to be taken home by each student, class photographs, and countless other materials. Occasionally, when this teacher has two students disturbing the class for any reason, at any time, reassignment of seats was made. It is done immediately without any student-teacher dialogue. The same strategy holds true for hall locker assignments. When a volatile situation arises or permanent record comments about two students who dislike one another, a change in hall lockers are made immediately.

One may challenge, "What's wrong with four or five children sitting together in a cluster? What's wrong with them helping one another?" Or, "What's wrong with children sitting in a circle with the teacher standing in the middle?" Experience has taught this teacher, with clusters, one student becomes the talker while the others assume the passive role as spectators. Also, children become easily distracted by their neighbor's quirks. In the circle situation the teacher continually has his back to half the circle and loses pupil eye contact. Sitting in rows make it easier for me to ask each and every child questions and to contribute to a problem at hand. Children go to the chalkboard to do a math problem. I expect every child to be prepared and to contribute and learn. When a child goes to the chalkboard and has difficulty, most assuredly several others in class have the same problem. By a series of questions the child completes the problem of his own accord. He has given birth to knowledge!

In mathematics, nothing is more frustrating than trying to teach fourth or fifth grade math and having children ignorant of their multiplication tables. At the beginning of my career, I did what most others do. I had my class start at page one of their math textbook, and go on from there. The whole year was frustrating to both the children and teacher because math at this grade level depends heavily on the multiplication tables. In my third year I began the school year giving a test on the different multiplication tables to indicate which tables each student was deficient. Each week we worked on two tables with children writing them down ten times each. Each day we had a contest. One day, for example, we had all boys on one side of the classroom with all the girls on the other. One child would ask another on the opposite side, "What is two times twelve?" If the response was wrong that child sat down. His homework assignment was to write "Two times twelve equals twenty four" ten additional times. If an opponent didn't answer correctly, he sat down and the child asking continued on to the next opponent. Eventually, one side won. The next day we would have rows one, two, and three, challenging rows four, five, and six. The teacher may suggest tournaments or even perhaps a special reward for the ultimate winner of the week. One reward I offered and was mentioned by former students twenty or thirty years later, was having a "Spooky Story." If my class deserved a reward, I would read a ghost story on Friday a half-hour before the end of school. I would darken the classroom by closing the curtains and shut off the ceiling electric lights. With the pitch-black classroom, I would lighten a candle that was inside a plastic skull. This enabled me enough light to read an Edgar Allan Poe mystery or some other short mysterious story. Occasionally, I would make a howling sound or tap the wooden desk as it related to the spooky story.

Those children who knew all their tables, from the ones through twelve times twelve, began work with their textbooks as well as learning Trachtenberg Math. This is a method of learning to multiply by adding numbers. It is a technique used in Switzerland.

Usually, we spend one month working on all tables from the ones through the twelfths, depending upon the progress and ability of the class, in general. At this time we begin with the math textbook. The author, oftentimes had three or four different ability groups. One group knew their tables and began work several weeks prior to this point in time. A second group completed the tables perhaps a week later. The third group took a week or two longer.

HOMEWORK

The most frustrating problem for a new teacher is assigning the proper amount of homework. Many parents have different philosophies. On more than a several occasions, a parent asked me mine. Many children are involved with all kinds of sports programs as well as ballet, cheerleading, Brownies, Cub Scouts, Indian Guides, church or synagogue meetings, and on and on. Excuses for a father's business trip, mother's card parties, and a million other excuses are some of the hindrances affecting homework assignments. Many times another teacher has assigned work to a child making the workload justifiably impossible to complete.

The importance of homework is twofold. First, it is a continuance of that day's classroom instruction and hopefully, a re-enforcement. Secondly, it develops a self-discipline necessary for the organization of learning and its structure lasting throughout a child's life.

PROCEDURE

On Monday's, I wrote the subjects and daily breakdown of homework assignments, on the chalkboard, for the complete week. I explained each subject's homework assignment. There is no excuse for being unprepared. When a child offered, "What if my dog eats my homework?" or "What if I lose it on the way to school?" With a "dead-pan" seriousness, my response was always, "There are only three acceptable excuses. If I die, you don't have to do your homework. If you die, you don't have to do your homework. And, God forbid, if either of your parents die, you don't have to do your homework."

If a child does not have the assignment a comment is made in my record grade book. That child is given a "grace" day accompanied by a remark, "You will complete the assignment tonight, or else." If the "or else" is necessary, the parent is contacted for an after school meeting as soon as possible. At the conference, the child is asked to tell his parent(s) why the assignment has not been completed. Any child that continues to have difficulty completing assignments is placed on my "every Friday afternoon conference with both child and parent(s)" agenda. A weekly oral report is given to the parent, welcoming the child's input. This technique has had excellent results because it reinforces the seriousness of completion of assignments and daily perseverance of the building blocks of learning.

MY TEACHING PHILOSOPHY

Teaching is the most exhausting, most exhilarating, most demanding, and the most rewarding of all professions. It is a way of life. It is also as sacred as the holy orders taken by a priest, rabbi, or minister. The classroom is my sanctuary and those placed in my care are my children.

Having said that, there is an invisible line between the students and myself. No matter what the rhyme or reason, that line is never crossed. Oftentimes a ten-year old girl feels my jacket pocket lid, or tie needs adjusting. This, I discourage as tactfully as I can. Tapping a child gently, on the head, or shaking a hand is my own self-imposed limits of personal contact. With boys, I sometimes extend a playful jab or pinched nose. At times, I may participate in a softball game or some other activity. Most children understand and accept their role as students and my role as their teacher. I am never a "buddy" to any child, including my own. I am their teacher and they are my pupils.

Foul language or throwing anything in the classroom is unacceptable behavior. Both actions result in the immediate dispatching of that particular child to the principal's office. In understanding proper classroom dynamics, novice teachers are sometimes misled by confused college professors. A few years ago I attended a graduate course at a local university. It was a education course in humanities designed to explore affective teaching techniques. At one session some students from an "alternative" high school spoke to us about the merits of being "unrestrained." They could smoke in class, call teachers by their first name, converse in whatever language suited them, and did whatever class work requested at their own convenience. When the students finished they dispersed from the center of the hall in all directions. I noticed one sixteen or seventeen-year old young lady pat her teacher on his buttocks.

We then gathered in small groups with several students assigned to each group. The purpose was to openly explore the thinking behind the alternative school's philosophy. After listening to polite rhetoric for several minutes, and unable to shake the familiarity just witnessed, I asked the young lady who displayed the questionable behavior, "Do any of the teachers take advantage of the students?" One member of our group disapproved of my question but the group leader thought it was acceptable. I repeated the question. The student replied, "I don't understand the question." I simplified the question, "Do male teachers fondle or sleep with the girls in your school?" The young lady looked at our group leader sheepishly then replied, "Some do."

The purpose of relating this experience is to indicate the invisible line separating student from teacher. It was violated in this "Alternative school."

Experience has confirmed the belief of beginning a school year being strict and demanding. A teacher may then choose to "ease up" come May or June. As a colleague once commented, "Give some children an inch in September and by June the administrators will have a replacement for you."

Teaching is the noblest of professions and to many, the most satisfying. A major conflict develops when a new teacher tries to be all things to all parents. The end result is the teacher in question loses sight of personal beliefs and philosophy. Try to develop your own method of classroom teaching techniques and procedure that is within the confines of your local school policy. Observe the "master" teachers who have survived and who are admired. Excellent judges are those who have graduated, and their parents. Don't let pride prevent you from asking questions no matter how naïve you may think they or you are. Be able to laugh at yourself.

Do you remember your favorite teachers? They were certainly not the ones who demanded little from you or had a classroom filled with turmoil and chaos. In those classes you now know you were cheated. Those teachers were inept. Those we admired most expected a great deal from us and were most demanding.

Always reach for the stars, and though we may never touch them, the children placed in our charge will certainly cherish the educational growth and personal experience they attained in the quest for academic excellence.

Teaching is a privilege and most times a joyous experience. There is both sadness and happiness at the end of a school year. The great joy of teaching is sharing life with the children you've taught. It has been helping them grow and having a better opportunity to achieve a fulfilling life. The sadness is that they are leaving you and the whole array of experiences with them has ceased.

OCTOBER

Back-To-School, Excuses, Nonsensical Frivolities

A principal usually greets parents on, "Back-to-School Night." He briefly outlines the school's general plans for that new school year. Highlights will include detailing the time schedule for student photographs, sweat shirt sales, poinsettias and geranium sales, cookie and cup cake sales, school and popular book and map sales, the Campbell Soup label collection, and several other money-raising events. Perhaps if you live in livestock country, they'll be a few events with the 4-H club and farming events. After this brief greeting, parents, armed with their child's daily class assignments, disperse to the school's classrooms. The session with each teacher is for approximately fifteen minutes.

The teacher's task is not to talk to individual parents but to outline the academic goals planned for the entire class for that academic school year. As a novice teacher, parents are unaware of your capabilities (or lack, if any). What you say and do is extremely critical at this stage of your career.

My method is to begin by writing my name, telephone number, and subject I teach on the chalkboard. The reason for this is oftentimes parents get lost and are in the wrong classroom. I detail the weekly routine of work on the chalkboard and explain how I have segmented the material into the ten months of the school year. In other words, I have a long range plan that encompasses the whole school year. Parents are informed that this plan is flexible, making allowances for the short month of November (Thanksgiving and Teacher Convention four-day weekends), as well as December (religious holidays). Parents are informed of my availability, anytime, at either school or at home. A rule of thumb example is offering a half-hour before my first class or after school for parent conferences or tutoring. If this is not convenient, I will travel to their home or they may bring their child to my home for tutoring. Excuses or obstacles are removed from preventing any child's maximum learning capabilities.

Parents are informed of my homework policy. Every parent is given the opportunity of selecting one of the following. If they select number one, they would like their child to do more homework than that assigned. Number two, agrees with the amount given. Number three would like their child to do every other problem assigned. Number four would like their child to do every fourth problem assigned, and finally, number five parents do not want their child to do any homework.

I conclude by stating anyone may hold me accountable if they select number one or two. They may not hold me accountable if they select any other number. I have found this method to be most effective in placating most parents.

CHILDREN LEAVING CLASS

You may have a parent complain about her child doing poorly in class whereas last year the same child received higher grades.

Every time a child leaves my class, I stop teaching and record the time and reason on a prepared roster. When the child returns to class, I stop teaching and record the time. Every Friday, after school, I tally the composite teaching time lost, for every child.

It is a useful means of countering any negative administrative ploy or parental concern whenever my teaching performance is questioned. The basic premise is that a child must be sitting in my classroom in order to learn. I am not a magician and cannot perform miracles instructing a child not present.

It is also my practice to keep an account, in the back of my lesson plan book, of recording the number of children tutored before or after school. Also recorded is any activity I performed that was above and beyond the call of duty. I place the date, the child's name and reason. Also included is any pertinent information, briefly stated with the date, that I believe should be noteworthy. At the end of the school year, when the administrator gives all teachers their annual performance observation evaluation sheet and a response is worthy to make, the times and dates I recorded throughout the school year are available. In the last ten years of teaching, many of my colleagues came to me for assistance when confronted with an administrative "problem." One superintendent called me, "Twenty page Filardo." He meant, for every page of any allegation or innuendo made against me, I responded with twenty pages detailing administrative ineptness or confusion. All this with the time, date, and reasons included.

CLASS PHOTOGRAPHS

October has been the month for taking individual as well as class photographs. A private company sets up shop on the stage of the auditorium or some large, vacant classroom. Classes are called on the intercom at a scheduled class time. Another interruption of teaching time! Each child is photographed as well as the teacher.

Class time is lost to take pictures, distribute the finished product, collect and account for monies received, and returned pictures not wanted. In addition, the photographer returns to school for retakes for those children who disliked the first set of pictures. The time lost is incalculable. It is especially annoying and time consuming since the school personnel are expected to be part time assistants to the whole operation.

GIFTED PROGRAMS

Many states and local school systems go through periods of trying to improve a mediocre school system's academic program. They rightfully see themselves drowning in a tide of mediocrity. Usually, central administration (the superintendent and his assistant), susceptible to any pilot program or gimmick proposed at some workshop, proposes an invalid idea and promotes its deliverance. After the Russian success with Sputnick, there was an outcry for more programs dealing with gifted and talented children. Opinions differed as to what the appropriate delivery system would be. It was personal experience to have several class members taken for five to ten hours per week. Those children missed more classroom instruction then they received in the media center. The standardized tests given to those excused from class indicated less academic growth per student than in previous years. Additionally, the potpourri offerings never were evaluated for validity or educational significance. I saw this ploy to extend the gifted and talented as a buckshot gimmick. Course offerings were not structured, organized building blocks courses of study. It had no means of evaluating what the children had learned, if anything. Another common fallacy is having the media center or library used as a meeting place or workshop. Knowledge is not transmitted by osmosis. Being near books will not automatically enrich the child.

The key to extending the gifted and talented child is having someone with an expertise specialized and excitedly instruct the child in a particular discipline. An artist doesn't haphazardly stroke a canvass, anywhere, with any color and expect a masterpiece. I have watched one of America's finest artists, Arthur Maynard, look at his canvas for long periods of time before placing his paint brush on the empty canvas. He then would stand back several feet and pondered his next stroke.

Wolfgang Amadeus Mozart was musically nurtured by his father, Leopold. Michelangelo served his apprenticeship under Ghirlandajo. With the master, Michelangelo studied the art of design and learned to work in colors. Thomas Edison, America's greatest genius, was home-schooled by his mother. Finally, in his letter to Robert Hooke in 1675, Sir Isaac Newton said, "If I see further, (than you and Decartes), it is by standing upon the shoulders of giants."

If given the choice, I favor special schools for the gifted and talented staffed by exceptional teachers similar to the Hunter

College Elementary School, the Bronx High School of Science, and Stuyvesant High School.

Personal experience of teaching a class of gifted children requires being prepared for the unexpected. The exceptional child has a catalytic affect upon his or her classmates as well as the teacher. In a heterogeneous class, oftentimes they are asked to help the slow child or assigned the "next ten pages."

On a personal level, I noticed my eldest son coming home from a sixth grade class depressed and exhausted. After continual probing, I found he was given the task of tutoring a classmate on how to tell time. Speaking to his teacher, I was informed tutoring was beneficial for my son's "social development."

My response was immediate and direct. All children are sent to school to become learned. They go to school, not to teach but to be taught. For "social development" most children attend church services, Boy or Girl Scouts, Little League sports, and other social activities. The school is suppose to have highly qualified personnel assigned to the task of helping children with learning disabilities. As a new teacher, or any other teacher, it is the horse that pulls the wagon. The wagon doesn't pull the horse.

NOVEMBER

Teacher Convention, Science Fair, Half-Days, Grades, Band

November, in New Jersey, usually has twenty-one actual days of school. It is a very short month. We have two, four-day weekends. The first is the New Jersey Education Association convention in Atlantic City. Two weeks later, we have the Thanksgiving holiday. Some schools also have a science fair.

The science fair is in the evening and all parents and friends are invited back to school. To the beginning or novice teacher, this is an excellent time to show the results of efforts working with your class. All parents love to view their children's work and confirm their, hopefully, high opinion of you, the teacher. If you've done your homework and perused textbook and teacher magazines, as well as respected "master teachers" for project ideas, you and your class projects should be ready.

If science has never been "your thing" may I strongly suggest attending such exciting seminars as the New Jersey Education Association's, "Good Ideas Conference," as well as the New Jersey State Math and Science Fairs? If you're not teaching in New Jersey perhaps your state has similar seminars. Join us in New Jersey, or you may want to start one yourself.

Another source of information would be the large corporations within your state that may have personnel available to assist you. At the seminars and fairs, the new teacher is tuned in with an exciting world. One exhibition witnessed a tie-in with a world gasoline shortage. The display had charts depicting petroleum coming from the earth, refined and shipped. The major gas suppliers have plenty of free material available for the asking.

Another project was aimed at energy conservation. Displays of wind energy, solar energy, and others were displayed. Parents will always appreciate an exuberant and updated effort. If the novice teacher is really anxious to do a good job, he or she may write or fax the Printing Office in Washington, D.C. for free information. The teacher may want to visit a Public Service Gas and Electric public relations office for available, free material. Sometimes, with a little coaxing, even the local post office will let you have some beautiful posters of famous people or events depicted to advertise different postage stamps.

A key source is the media center or library. Today, they not only have files and current magazine articles, but also computer software and printing services. The areas and contacts available are almost limitless.

N.J. EDUCATION ASSOCIATION

Back in the old days, some two or three decades ago, the convention was a blustery cold event that forced many teachers to stay in the convention hall or spend a great deal of time in their hotel room. Atlantic City, in November, feels like Siberia. The teachers spent a day checking out numberless table displays and come home with several shopping bags full of free samples. Lectures were interesting and less political. I still remember one lecture, in 1961, given by Dr. Patrick Suppes, of Stanford University. He was excited about the advent of computers and their affect upon education. Most teachers attending his lecture were skeptical. Today, we see fruition of that lecture. Some schools have subject matter broken down into concepts and stored by computers. Investigation into the future affect of computers in foreign languages is also amazing. Dr. Suppes prophesied the chains of restraint will finally be broken as far as preventing our children from advancing or remaining at the level they are capable of. The future of education is boundless with intelligent leadership. Imagine our future language classes speaking directly to children in a foreign country with both classes connected electronically.

Another very important aspect of our teacher association is that its most important reason for being, is our professional protection. Alone, we pose no threat and are easy victims of misguided board of education trustees, inept administrators, or confused parents. As one of the more than 150,000 members, our association has always been there to support us in our greatest hour of need. It has been my experience that more than a few teachers have not been rehired because of some triviality or difference of opinion with a dunderhead administrator. A untenured teacher, was asked to change the grades of two students. Their parents were on the board of education. The students had received a "C" grade in physics. When the teacher refused, feeling the grades given were just, the principal reminded the teacher he lacked tenure. The teacher thought about that threat for several minutes, then responded, "If I have to work under those conditions, I quit."

The shocked principal responded, "You can't quit in January. The contract reads you must notify the board sixty days before you leave."

The teacher replied, "We'll split the difference. I'm history in thirty days." With that, he left teaching and became an outstanding space, electrical engineer with Rockwell International in California.

For those who have entered the wrong profession, the administration has three years to appraise all new teachers. When the public complains about a "poor" teacher I always think that both the poor teacher and the administrator(s) who hired that teacher should be fired. Teachers do not hire themselves.

Tenure is important and our state organization is there to protect us from losing it. In more than forty years of teaching, I can honestly say the pendulum leans heavily against us. So, novice teacher, by all means be a supportive member of your teacher association. I have always been grateful for their support and encouragement. This teacher is forever thankful for all the benefits and highly qualified personnel assisting him throughout his career.

HALF-DAY SESSIONS

Some school districts have half-day sessions. These are five days in which children have half days of school. After lunch or snack time, scheduled conference, with parents, fill up the second half of the school day. At the parent-teacher conferences of fifteen minutes, the teacher hands the parent the child's report card. It is another critical time for the novice teacher to be prepared to support any grade given to any child. Some parents will try to tell you why their child is having difficulty.

I remember a situation in my first year of teaching. During a difficult arithmetic test, a ten-year old girl left her seat and went to the classroom window to look at "the birds." I asked her if she was ill. She replied she wasn't ill. Last year's teacher gave her permission to go to the window anytime she was uncomfortable or bored. Needless to say she was instructed to return to her seat. The same child cheated during a spelling exam. She was given a homework assignment of explaining the problem along with a parental signature.

The classroom I taught in was on the ground level, overlooking a parking lot. On this half-day session, I happened to look out the window and noticed a car bolt into a parking space just outside my window. The mother leaped out of the car, slammed the door, and bolted into my classroom. Her first abrasive question, "Mr. Filardo, what is your philosophy of education?" At that moment I felt I was still back at college responding to some professor's question in a course, "The Fundamentals of Teaching, 101."

After our tense dialogue, I had my first experience chatting with our superintendent. He had received a telephone call from this upset mother. At the end of the school year, the same mother was most cordial and grateful for her daughter's substantial educational growth and corrected school behavior.

At half-day sessions you should have pertinent comments written down in your marking book alongside the child's name. The teacher should have test scores in every subject taught and also extra credit contributions each child has made, if any. Truthful and positive comments soften your critical statements. Checking back to the child's permanent record, see if your appraisal of the child's performance and overall abilities agree or disagree with the previous teacher's comments. Many times a parent will mention something that happened "last year." Be honest and sincere with parents and certainly tactful. Never forget you are a civil servant and in essence, work for the parents of all the children you teach. Loving parents know their child. If a child has been careless with written assignments ask the parent to act as a screening agent. Parents are informed of children have homework everyday but Friday, Saturday, and Sunday. If there is no written work all children should review all that has happened in the five hours of school. Advise the parents to set up a daily time when the child is expected to go to a quiet place of study. Be sure there is no radio, television, pets, friends, or any other distraction when a child studies. That hour is strictly set aside for study and review. There are virtually no common sense exceptions. My response to, "I have no place to study," excuse is, as a young boy in East Harlem, I would have to study in a vacant bathroom. It was the only place available in our three room apartment having a brother, sister, and mother.

With my own children, I found the first week or two difficult in developing or re-establishing positive study habits. Once a child adjusts to the routine of studying and reaping the rewards of better grades, rebellion slowly ebbs away. The vast majority of mothers, however, are the key to sticking to this daily routine. She is and has always been the heart of her family.

Weekly oral reports with parent and child are offered to those children who have difficulty following the usual class routine and assignments. The time slot for conferences is every Friday, just after the closing bell. With the parent and child, I reviewed the pluses and minuses of the child's work for that particular week. My belief is there is no excuse for a lack of educational growth, with all things being equal.

The importance of the weekly Friday parental visit is primarily designed to correct poor study habits. Thinking as a child, "My mother will see the teacher, yell at me and forget about everything tomorrow. I'll just keep doing things my way." With the weekly conference we have a constant, never-ending accountability because we both love the child and want to correct bad study and homework habits. This, the child begins to understand. That is why we both have taken the time to help him or her learn. Even the child tires of hearing a repetition of the same excuses of not doing the assigned tasks. While we know there are sometimes legitimate excuses for not completing every single assignment, those become the exception to the rule and are made with great reluctance.

GRADES

As a novice teacher my rationale was that of an adult. If I gave a child an "F" or failure, I thought the child would go home and try harder to improve the failing grade. The fact was, I found, the opposite to be true. When I gave a child an "F" the child usually thought, "My teacher knows all the answers and if he thinks I'm stupid than I must be stupid! Why try?"

This personal philosophy changed my second year of teaching. Grades should never be used as a weapon or threat but rather as a means of encouragement helping the educational growth of a child. Another way of looking at an "F" is to understand it means a child has been in your class for about two months and has learned absolutely nothing. That is impossible! In no stretch of anyone's imagination is that possible unless the child is deaf, has a deep-seated mental problem, or the teacher is a real clinker! All children in my class have to participate. If they give a wrong answer, then its my job to probe and keep probing for the correct answer with less difficult questions leading to the correct response. If this procedure, as well as any others you may use, has taken place daily for two months, I know the child has learned something.

There have been children, from my first year of teaching, I thought would never live productive lives. If asked about any one of them I most assuredly would have replied, "Make it? Are you kidding? See that kid over there? He can't even find the door to the boy's bathroom!" Years later, the same children became the town's mayor, doctor, and local lawyer. Yep! Even two of my teaching colleagues were those flunky kids! The lesson learned was that only God knows what someone will eventually become. I have neither the ability nor the foresight to predict or prejudge anyone's future. Many non-educational factors contribute to what we all ultimately become. Think back to the turning points in your life. Think back to someone dear to you and the impact they've had on your life. Well?

School Band and Music Instruction

Many elementary and secondary schools have a band. Children that play an instrument also take music lessons during the school day. Most schools have a Christmas/Hanukkah Concert and a Spring Concert, usually in April. Children will need to rehearse and be taken from your classroom. The bottom line question is, "What do I do with those children remaining in my class if more than a few take music lessons?"

We had 550 students in the high school, grades nine through twelve. There were 1,450 children in the lower grades. The school was never noted for academic excellence. One major factor was the amount of classroom time lost by children involved in the following performing groups at the high school level. We have: wind ensemble, symphonic band, jazz ensemble, flute trio, clarinet sextet, saxophone trio, brass quartet, brass choir, the orchestra, string trio, string quartet, concert choir, chorale ensemble, super six, thunderbirds, and drama club.

In the middle school, grades six through eight, we have a senior band, junior band, the orchestra, senior jazz band, junior jazz band, 7th & 8th grade chorus, and the 6th grade chorus.

At the fourth and fifth grades there is a 5th grade band, beginner band, jazz band, the orchestra, 5th grade choir, and 4th grade choir.

At the combined third grade level we have a 3rd grade choir. Staff wise, there are eight faculty members in the music department, one known as the dramatics arts faculty member, six fine arts faculty members as well as two listed as practical arts faculty. The total members of the faculty, seventeen.

The annual school budget for 2,000 children exceeds $27 million dollars. There is a major fallacy we keep reading about,

"The more money spent on education, the better education children will receive."

Martin Katzman, of the Harvard-MIT Joint Center for Urban Studies, and an economist said, "Increasing school costs may be a sign of gross operating inefficiency, as they often are in private industry. The amount a school spends is less important than how wisely they spend it."

November is an excellent time to tighten up loose teaching ends. Prepare a folder that includes materials to help those in need of re-enforcement or extension. It may be a construction-type aid. For example, several children have difficulty understanding place value in arithmetic. Cut out a rectangular piece of oak tag measuring twelve inches by four inches. Four circles are cut measuring two inches across the diameter. Each circle is numbered zero through nine and written similar to the numbers on a clock. All the numbers are equidistant from one another. In the rectangular oak tag four half-inch holes are strategically located so that only one number from each circular disc will show. Then attach each disc with a small brass fastener enabling the disc to rotate. Starting above the top right hole write "ones" then "tens" over the second hold, followed by "hundreds" then on the extreme left, "thousands." Sitting with the children needing extra help the teacher could review the skill by asking each child to register the number asked on their place value aid. Once learned, the children advance to the same type place value aid, but instead of "ones," "tens," and "hundreds," we advance to "thousands," "ten thousands," and "hundred thousands."

Also included in your folder there could be brief outlines for a class-play. In our reading and language arts textbooks, we had several stories about Greek Mythology. Children are fascinated by the ancient myths and enjoyed the supplemental filmstrips and tapes. We decided to video-tape six scripts, These were: Baucis and Philemon (my favorite), Eurydice and Orpheus, Daphne and Apollo, The Trojan War, Perseus and Medusa, and Echo and Narcissus.

It took us six months to write the scripts and get them produced. Letter writing is another popular class activity. Names and addresses of people and corporations were given to the children. The letters were mailed to places offering free material. Our children received everything from pictures of baseball, football, basketball, and hockey stars to wooden nickels from a bank in Utah.

Another letter writing activity was placing letters written by our children in waxed sealed plastic bottles. A parent, vacationing in West Palm Beach, Florida, agreed to take two cases of sealed, letter filled plastic bottles and toss them off a boat at least twenty miles from the Florida coastline. We wanted the bottles to be caught in the Gulf of Mexico stream and taken across the Atlantic Ocean to Europe.

Children performing in the band or receiving music instruction have the same opportunity when the chorus and chorale children leave the classroom. Difficulty arises when a student is involved in several other activities.

One child wrote a letter to a school in Alaska and received an Eskimo Cookbook from Shishmaref. The recipes in the Eskimo Cookbook were the talk of the school. They included, Lincod Eskimo Ice Cream, Tomcod Liver and Berries, and delicious Soured Seal Liver.

During a disruption of teaching time, we have also built short-wave radio Heath kit receivers, bird houses, and marionettes for our play, "Beauty and the Beast." Please keep in mind the activities mentioned did not all happen in one school year.

The difficult problem faced is having children return to necessary structured lessons when band, instrumental music lessons, chorus, and chorale sessions are over. The most productive teaching time is in the morning when children are most alert and well rested. The further into the school day and school week, the more tired and shorter the child's interest span. This teacher, as well as many of his colleagues have urged class interruptions be scheduled for late afternoons, preferably on Fridays. Our greatest blunder is to have an assembly, physical education, art, music, and band scheduled within the first two hours of any school day.

SWEAT SHIRT SALES

Many schools have more than their share of "do-gooders." These are parents, usually mothers, who sincerely want to help. Unfortunately, their well-intended ideas and gimmicks become extra workloads for others and disturbs the learning process. The sale of school sweat-shirts is a perfect example. Their goal is to raise money for the school media center or band or some other noble cause. Office personnel are asked to type up the advertisement and application forms. They are reproduced on the school Xerox machine, using school paper, school personnel, and blocking the teacher's usage of equipment and school daily operations. Children are sent to the office (missing class work), to pick up copies of advertisement for distribution to all children. The teacher is forced to stop teaching to distribute the material and collect monies each day for about a week. We have trouble with children losing cash or checks, teachers losing slips and/or checks and monies, and the beat goes on. Children are sent to the office each day with the applications and money. Office personnel have to record transactions and place the money in a school safe. Sweat-shirts are then given to the child who in turn distributes them to the children in class. Wrong sizes are returned to the office and the beat goes on. The "do-gooder" has contributed, maybe, one hundred dollars. Children have lost valuable classroom learning time, never recovered. Teacher time wasted, salary-wise, runs into thousands of dollars, not to mention all the office personnel and school materials used.

As a novice teacher, you should expect to be collecting money for many causes. A positive suggestion would be to have handy Xerox forms in your top desk drawer containing the names of all children in your class. Beside each name, it may be a good idea to have the parent's name and telephone number. Also on the same sheet of paper include columns for money received or items collected or distributed. Never leave any money or wallet or pocketbook in your desk or unlocked closet. Always send collected money to the school office immediately after it is collected. Make it a practice to lock your classroom door when your children are in some other classroom or gymnasium.

More than a few teachers have had money taken from them needlessly. Children have also had items taken from their desk when a classroom is vacant. Always remind children to leave valuables at home or in their locked hall lockers. My classroom students are told not to bring dice, cards, knives, computers, dolls, radios, tapes, guns, or anything else that does not belong in school. One fifth grade boy, several years ago, received a great deal of attention bringing to school centerfolds of Playboy magazine and pasting them on the inside doors of the enclosed compartments of the stalls in the boy's bathroom. The only way I found out was investigating the sudden rash of boys wanting to be excused to go to the bathroom. At first I thought we had some serious diarrhea epidemic from the school lunches. Listening to my colleagues mention the same problem, during lunch, led a natural path to the boy's room for a closer investigation.

DECEMBER

Observations, Tests, Post Conferences, Violent/ Frequently Absent Children, Parties

TEACHER OBSERVATIONS

Most administrative manuals define a principal as, "One whose main function is to improve the quality of education." In order to accomplish that task it is necessary for the administrator to observe teachers and make, hopefully, constructive suggestions. Almost all teachers become a little apprehensive when an administrator observes their class. Most administrators have been teachers and are or should be aware of the human feelings involved. The novice teacher should take careful pains to have a prepared lesson plan.

This is not a time for experimentation or the time for a democratic, unrestrained outburst of pupil dynamics unless the administrator openly advocates that mentality and is a swinger. Principals usually want to see a learning environment. Most want to see a healthy situation with order and full class participation.

Few known administrators approve of gum-chewing, comic book reading, game-playing, inattentiveness and any other sophomoric behavior. Bulletin boards should be updated and wall charts, along with posted pictures, should be secured properly without graffiti. Children desks should be reasonably clean and in order without paper and books dangling out from them. Objectives for a particular lesson should be noted in your lesson plan book. A sheet of paper with a brief outline of that particular day's lessons would be a much-needed aid for those who may be nervous. Oftentimes an administrator may request seeing your lesson plan book before observing your class performance. It would be a good idea to plan a special activity or science experiment to reinforce your objectives of that lesson. Always keep the objectives of the lesson in mind. The involvement of children is always expected. One glaring fault many new teachers are guilty of is, in their anxiety to do well and make a positive impression is lecturing throughout the observation with little or no student input.

During one teacher observation in a social studies class, a child volunteered and displayed a corporation stock certificate. The child explained the concept of the lesson. The observation went well and most children understood the objectives of that lesson.

The main teacher performance area is termed "Instructional Skills." These are measured by planning and organization, appropriateness of materials, resourcefulness and adaptability, ability to motivate, use of resources, classroom techniques, parent relationships and student relationships.

Under management ability, you must be aware of your relationship with pupils, discipline, and personal efficiency.

Your administrator must also evaluate your professional responsibility. He or she will appraise your commitment, staff relations, out-of-class responsibilities, and your ethics.

On your personal qualities, you will be evaluated on your appearance, speech, attitude, and judgment. Several years ago, a beginning teacher came to school with an extremely short skirt. When checking in, she stooped to pick up a piece of dropped mail. The principal observed the teacher and suggested she go home and replace her skirt with a "more appropriate one."

One of the most common negative comments heard is about the teacher's personal appearance. I have witnessed female teachers wearing very suggestive clothing. Males sometimes wear tight fitting trousers and open shirts. It is not uncommon to see men with earrings and hair tied in a knot, resembling Thomas Jefferson.

One does not fault another's lifestyle, "per se." The primary question is, "Does a particular lifestyle make learning more difficult for the children placed in your care?"

POST-OBSERVATION CONFERENCE

Two or three days following your observation you will receive three copies from the principal with his findings. A post observation conference follows a day later. After this meeting comments are suggested on the typewritten observation report you are requested to sign. The principal keeps one copy, the superintendent receives a copy, and you keep the third.

For the non-tenured teacher I would suggest not doing too much talking unless the observation report is totally unjustified. In that case you might suggest another observation. If this is unacceptable to the administrator then the non-tenured teacher has one of two choices. You may accept the findings and hope to be rehired, or respond to each and every criticism with facts, not opinions. What were the objectives of the lesson observed? What techniques did you employ to carry out those objectives? How do your bulletin boards, charts, and other displays support the subject observed? What preceded the lesson and what followed the lesson critiqued?

Personal denials of what was written may be soul cleansing but it does little else and works against you. Remember, right or wrong, the administrator is right. Bite the bullet or ride out into the sunset.

Finally, I have found it a very good practice to save any and all correspondence from school personnel and parents. File it chronologically. Seven months later an observation or some other matter may surface. A favorable comment made by a school administrator or parent may support your position in a current matter. Always remember to stick to the facts.

THE VIOLENT CHILD

Nothing is more upsetting than to have an emotionally disturbed child in your class. The child is mentally sick and needs special care. Uncontrollable behavior violates the learning rights of all other children and hinders learning. I had one such child I will never forget. It was the most frustrating teaching year I had ever experienced. The child physically struck three teachers with a bicycle chain, and punched two other teachers, including me. On the playground the ten-year old boy attempted to strangle a female classmate. The young lady had an impression of his fingerprints on her neck. Investigation of the child's permanent record indicated similar trouble in every grade and a regression of learning according to the standardized test scores recorded. Referrals to the Child Study Team proved fruitless. At one point the psychologist asked me to define written reports submitted and what I meant by "emotionally disturbed." I gave an example of one person stabbing another. When the response was, "Did the knife blade penetrate the skin?" Our dialogue, at that point, abruptly ended. I was becoming emotionally disturbed by such lunacy.

The disturbed child, in question, was later picked up by the police for placing a knife blade to the neck of a newspaper boy. He demanded the paper collection money. After a court hearing, the boy was sent to the state diagnostic center for observation and treatment. Fifteen years later, my emotionally disturbed student was shot and killed by the local police for aiming a rifle at one police officer.

I hope you, the beginning teacher, will never have the tragic experience of trying to teach an emotionally disturbed youngster. If you do, the first recourse is to be on record with your principal, nurse, and the Child Study Team. It would be smart to notify all school personnel mentioned, with a typewritten letter. Be sure to keep a carbon copy for your own future reference. If you fear for your life, my suggestion would be to contact your state teacher representative. In our case, it is the very supportive New Jersey Education Association's regional office. With the tenured teacher, my first reaction is to contact the local police department. The main fear with the above-mentioned child was that he was going to kill himself or someone else. In this particular case, the ten-year old boy fell through the cracks.

THE FREQUENTLY-ABSENT CHILD

The most difficult child to teach is the one who isn't present in the classroom. One year I had a child who was absent thirty of the first forty-eight days of school. Checking her permanent record I discovered the child had missed more than one hundred eighty days of school during her first four years. I alerted the principal and the Child Study Team. The days the child came to school was intolerable for both the child and teacher. One day, out of sheer frustration, I exclaimed, "I am not Jesus or Moses. I cannot perform miracles. I'm just a simple teacher. You must come to school to learn!" Early the next morning the child's mother came to school and the first thing she asked, "Is it true that you told my daughter you were Jesus Christ?" I laughed and responded, "She even got that wrong!"

Continued referrals to the authorities resulted in the child being removed from my class. She continued her absenteeism, and was moved on to the sixth grade. The beginning teacher will one day realize as much as they would like to be able to teach and reach every child, there are a few who will slip through the cracks.

In analyzing a child's permanent record I glance at the number of days a child has missed school in previous years. There is a correlation between a troubled student and a high number of days absent. An exception being a child with a severe medical problem who has had home instruction.

No one can teach or be held accountable for an empty classroom seat. The solution to any problem is first to find the source. Speak with your principal, Child Study Team, nurse, and the child's parent(s) and try to improve the situation.

CHILD STUDY TEAM

In one graduate course a professor stated, "In all the years I've been a teacher, principal, and superintendent, I have never seen a school psychologist help one child. What they do is read a referral sent to them. They then find the appropriate response letter in their files. After filling in the child's name they elongate on what the teacher has said."

At the time I shrugged in disbelief. Later, what the learned Dr. Joseph Priestly said was the truth. While the psychologist does test the child, usually for some fifteen minutes, every other week, is it effective? Is it like trying to fill a bottomless bottle? One psychologist suggested giving the troubled child M&M candies or cookies in an attempt at behavior modification. This teacher's response to the psychologist was similar to Pavlov's theory of ringing a bell every time a dog is fed. More importantly, the other children seeing a teacher give M&M candies to one child to try and modify his behavior wonder why they don't receive any candy. Perhaps they too, should misbehave to get some candy or cookies. Common sense would favor a psychiatrist treating disturbed children and placing them in an environment conducive to aiding their abnormal behavior.

It would be sound advice for the novice teacher to support the current system. Inwardly, you may want to convince yourself of finding a better way of helping the emotionally disturbed child. If you decide to fight the system, forget about tenure, you're history.

CHORUS AND CHORALE

Children taken out of class for the Christmas/Hanukkah Concert and the Spring Concert lose one or two hours of instruction per week. This amounts to approximately eight or nine hours in the usual month of rehearsals. It is uncommon for a whole class to be part of the school chorus. The new teacher can do little but bear the inconvenience and try to suggest a tie-in song selection(s) to correspond with classroom subjects. I have benefited by a positive relationship with the elementary school music teacher on a few occasions. In studying the Civil War, my children were taught to sing Dixie, Battle Hymn of the Republic, Eating Goober Peas, John Brown's Body, and several others. In the same year we utilized those songs with a video-taped production of the Battle of Bull Run.

The novice teacher can turn what is a gross waste of time, into a means of supplementing a future activity. The chorale group pull out is usually made on a smaller scale and leaves the teacher an opportunity to re-organize to compliment such time wasted. The growing frustration of children missing class for just "one or two classes" dramatically increases with the passing weeks of the school year. The tragedy is having children miss ten to fifteen school days per year involved in nonsensical frivolities.

POINSETTIA FLOWER SALE

Another popular time-waster experienced is the Christmas/Hanukkah money-raiser and time-consuming Poinsettia Flower Sale. Usually it is a school mother "do-gooder" that has a "flower calling." The school office becomes a florist depot to some while others equate it to a funeral parlor. The school main office is decorated with flower pots on every shelf and table top. Advertisements fill the teacher's mailbox. Teachers and office personnel now have money responsibilities of collecting, keeping an accounting of plants and money both purchased and returned. All this is added on to just days before the holiday recess and growing anxieties.

CHRISTMAS AND HANUKKAH PARTIES

Children love parties! Between the excitement of the gift-giving and a two week upcoming school vacation, the tempo of school life begins building about the beginning of the second week in December. In direct contrast, with the escalating thoughts of partying, seriousness of classroom learning declines. The classroom door resembles the swinging bar room door seen in the old cowboy movies. Children leaving for band rehearsals, chorus, flower sales, food collections for the needy, elfing (that is, fifty odd children wearing elf costumes and parading the school corridors extending anyone and everyone good wishes.) All this plus many other demands fuel the flames of euphoria. In one school we even had some hall revelers dress up like Santa Claus and his wife giving out candy canes.

The best laid lesson plans take second place to the sales and assembly programs ranging from the school plays having little to do with subject matter, to a Christmas/Hanukkah band and chorus extravaganza. The last one this teacher experienced even included Ravel's "Bolero." I had a great deal of difficulty associating the "Bolero" with the birth of Christ or even Santa Claus. These are the times that try any teacher's sanity.

Collecting party money, as well as placating your class mother and her party plans oftentimes becomes hectic. Most schools have rules that limit the amount of money a child may spend on a gift bag present. Every year the teacher should expect to have some boy receive a girl's gift or the other way around. Teachers are usually told by the principal, to be sure all holiday decorations on the walls and door have been removed before leaving for the holiday vacation.

After a week needed to recuperate, it may be a good idea for the novice teacher to re-appraise lesson plans for the remaining part of the school year. The areas or activities should be adjusted. Very few lesson plans are exactly on target after approximately fourteen weeks of school. January is a month of five weeks providing time to coordinate all subject matter at all individual grade levels.

TESTS

You will think about the tests you give. What is the purpose of a test? A beginning teacher may be slightly confused as to the purpose of a test. When I give a test, the fact is I'm testing both the children and myself. If half the class does poorly on a test, an indication may be I did a poor job getting the material across to my children. Perhaps the reason was too many interruptions with nonsensical frivolities, too many parties, or whatever. Perhaps it's me! Did I ignore the amount of time children missed class and just barged ahead anyway? If so, then I goofed! Let's back up and try covering the same material more slowly and in depth. Let's go over the most common mistakes made. Where did I miss the boat? How many children missed the same question?

On the other hand, if most of the class tested well, then I feel like the greatest teacher in the world! Better than the greatest, even better than Socrates! Tests are important and this teacher makes every effort possible to write something positive alongside every child's test grade. My children know a perfect paper always has the word, "EXCELLENT." A grade of "B" or "B+" has the word, "SUPER" or "GREAT!" If a child receives the grade "C," "D," or "F," the comment will be, "COULD DO BETTER," or "DID YOU STUDY?"

Parents are required to sign all test papers and I welcome any remark or request of a parent/teacher conference. Oftentimes a parental remark justifies a poor grade and a child is permitted a retest. Every teacher should try to make testing a positive part of schoolwork.

JANUARY

Professional Problems, Administrators, Handwriting

LONGEST MONTH

After the Christmas/Hanukkah winter vacation break both teachers and children should settle in for the longest and most productive school month. Winter storms and high absenteeism set aside, this month could set the goals that will dovetail into the final week of the school year.

PROFESSIONAL PROBLEMS

A beginning teacher may ask, "What are some of the problems should I be aware of?"

The experienced, tenured teacher would offer some of the following annoyances. Our preparation periods are sometimes compromised when we're asked to cover some other teacher's class. It could be an emergency situation or perhaps a spur of the moment meeting or parent conference. When staff members are asked to cover another's class that teacher loses a conference period or break from duties. It is especially annoying if you had planned to run off some class Xerox material or perhaps make a telephone call to some parent. The school calendar may be arbitrarily changed so that only two days would be allowed during the normal week's Spring vacation. These have been set aside for parent conferences.

Another obstacle happens when our input on an important issue is not taken seriously. This usually happens when we're asked to serve on a committee. Teachers are usually unwilling to participate on committees because of a lack of released time and serious consideration of the teacher's input. For example, I was asked to be on a math committee to help select a textbook for the following school year. Our committee of seven teachers screened thirteen different math books with representatives from each publishing house. After spending four months on this committee we discovered our principal had already ordered the textbooks before receiving our selection. They were discovered stacked at the back of our stage in the auditorium.

Many teachers feel participation is merely tokenism. In fact, some administrators have a solution to a problem but in order to prevent any professional fall out, select teachers to an "Ad Hoc" committee. Hopefully, the hand picked committee will arrive at the same conclusion and agree with the solution the administrator already had in mind. The findings are presented to the board of education for approval. If the solution proves successful, the administrator glows. If, however, the reverse is true, all fingers point to the members on the "Ad Hoc" shortsighted committee. It's a win-win situation for the administrator.

Many teachers, including this teacher, have always been sensitive to dichotomous administrative and trustees rulings and directives. Some teachers receive a leave of absence while others are denied, without an explanation.

Another problem, in many schools, is the lack of private teacher/parent telephones. It is highly unprofessional to have a telephone in the teachers' room trying to discuss a student's problem with a parent. Other teachers, janitors, computer repair personnel, and school guests/visitors are talking, eating, or just listening while personal problems are discussed.

It is questionable for central administration (superintendent and his assistants), to change a student's grade on a report card. Oftentimes it happens in a student's senior year, just before graduation. Experience indicates many teachers are upset and greatly annoyed at the superintendent's lack of intestinal fortitude and lack of supporting his teachers.

Complaints are often heard about some superintendent wanting a doctor's note after a teacher's absence. One incident experienced was a superintendent not coming to work after a snowfall. Although all children and teachers were expected to be at school on time he didn't arrive until three hours later. It so happened a senior boy's car skidded off the road and crashed, injuring the boy. When the boy's parent called to speak to the superintendent she discovered he was not in school because of the weather.

Another factor that needs addressing is whether school aides should be helping teachers or become inundated with work given to them by the principal. It is usually some public relations gimmick or fund-raiser planned activity. Many teachers are concerned about the many interruptions caused by the school's classroom intercom messages. We are continually bombarded with messages of collection of monies for multiple gimmicks, or of distributing flyers. Many of us feel the public relations agenda, especially evident at school election and budget time, in most schools is overbearing.

SUPERINTENDENTS

January is also a fine time to think about administrators. At an early stage in your career you will find, just as all roads at one time led to Rome, so too, all problems lead to the office of the superintendent. The hiring of a superintendent is the one most important function of the board of education. With a recent survey indicating a less than a four year job expectancy rate, the revolving door syndrome is an ever-present chief administrator's fact of life.

The discouraging aspect of all this is, with every new face comes a changing educational philosophy. Looking back at this revolving door, I can honestly say we have had only one very able and knowledge chief administrator in forty-one years. Of fifteen superintendents this teacher has experienced we had several tyrants. We also had an alcoholic. Several years ago the board hired a misogynist, who loved to see female teachers cry in his office. Teachers also contended with an "invisible man" from Harvard. He was the only person I ever witnessed cutting his grass with a lawn mower dressed in a suit with a white shirt and tie. Another, best described as a dirty old man, believed our school was his harem and had slept with several female teachers. Included in this array of misfits included a fanny-grabber (both male and female), and several plain, simple country bumpkins.

The greatest tragedy is the fact that school districts leave the hiring of the new superintendent to some outside agency. Plain and simple, that board of education action indicates a tremendous lack of intestinal fortitude and a shirking of an electorate's responsibility. The hiring agency knows or cares little of your community. The newly hired superintendent, wanting to impress, embarks on a course of action. The severity of this initial act or series of acts by the superintendent determines the force of staff actions which is directly linked to the longevity of that person in the new school system. It is much easier to fire the coach than to replace the whole team, especially if they're tenured.

The majority of the top "500" major corporations in America are structured and promote personnel from within their organizations. They know the caliber of their personnel and the sensitivity of the corporate structure. If a school has two assistant superintendents, promote from within their school staff, when a vacancy occurs the system has a feed-in line of succession. This teacher has taught under thirty-six administrators on all levels. Nothing is more demoralizing than to see a constant flow of inept, flunky administrators swinging in and out like the ticks of a metronome. It is demoralizing because most of the teaching staff realizes the continued vacillation of questionable leadership impacts directly on the children. Additionally, this action indicates to the teaching staff and community there is no one capable to lead the school from within the current school personnel. If that is the case, than that particular school district is mediocre, at best.

Most superintendents are involved with public relations tied-in with their school budgets. Very few are concerned with or even know their staff, with few exceptions. Most chief administrators remain close to their office and seldom venture into the main stream of the school's learning environment unless there is some kind of event and a newspaper photographer. This teacher remembers having a new superintendent and being invited into his office. He asked me about my homework policy. When told of my method and procedure, he thought it was fair. It seems a parent, being a part time real estate saleswoman, asked to see him. Under the guise of complaining about her child receiving too much homework, tried to sell the superintendent a house.

The top administrator should have been a master teacher and able to identify the important teaching techniques of his staff. He or she should be able to infuse valid ideas and workable suggestions into his district. These positive abilities warrant a loyal and disciplined staff. The upper most goal of any superintendent should be a never-ending quest of academic excellence for all children, all the time.

More than a few school administrators offer little more than handshakes, backslapping, and the ability to give joyous parties. They also noted for being quick picking up the tab. Their main goal is to have a tranquil operation and a happy family. It is a rare experience to find a superintendent contributing to excellence or even change the time consuming gimmicks. The superintendent will react to community's unrest.

This teacher remembers a superintendent rejecting his faculty's suggestion of exploring the possibility of sharing and exchanging teachers with a nearby school district. The purpose was to infuse new teaching techniques and ideas to both involved schools.

Several years ago, I remember meeting with a superintendent. He asked if I had criticized the modern math textbook. I said I did because both teachers and their children didn't understand the material of sets and subsets. His next question was, "Aren't you happy with the amount of money you're making?"

The quick response was, "What does that have to do with our children not understanding the material and our teachers not knowing how to teach it?" End of the confrontation.

Another superintendent chastised the athletic department for violating a rule of issuing one football player, equipment one day before he should have. The youngster, unknowingly picked up his uniform August 31st instead of September 1st. Our chief administrator screamed, "It's morally wrong. We may get into big trouble with the State Department." It was common knowledge this same married man was a notorious womanizer. He had been spending most nights at a teacher's house with his car parked in her driveway. Talk about morals?

More often than not a superintendent knows little about a novice teacher unless the school district is extremely small. His input comes from a principal and perhaps several parents. At the beginning of the school year's orientation, you should take a good look at your superintendent. It'll probably be the only time you'll see him or her. Unless, of course, you create a serious problem and receive an urgent request to meet in the oval office.

PRINCIPAL

It is the belief of many teachers in undergraduate and graduate school, principals, for the most part, were "master teachers" that come up from the district's ranks. Bunk! Close observation and general discussions at local and national conventions, find it is the exception and not the rule in most school districts.

A common occurrence of filling a vacant administrative, most often, is filled by a close friend of the chief administrator or that of a board member. The individual's credentials or teaching experience runs a poor second. A card playing, and bowling alley buddy of an administrator was screened for a vacancy. Two hundred candidates were also interviewed. Late one evening, the local buddy gets a telephone call, slips on his trousers and meets with the local board of education. The superintendent's buddy scored a "strike" and became principal. So much for Ivy League credentials.

Another filled administrative vacancy witnessed a teacher having three years experience teaching half the fifth grade subjects. By chance he sang in the church choir with the superintendent and his wife. When the vacancy occurred, he sang his way into the job. Some districts have been known to fill administrative vacancies from pressures placed upon them by the town mayor, council members, or board trustees.

Another popular path to the becoming a principal seems to be the guidance department. Perhaps a close proximity of both offices has something to do with the golden brick road.

Experience indicates principals are also guilty of spending an extraordinary amount of time dealing with public relations. It is a rare principal that observes a teacher and offers one or several positive suggestions on how a single lesson could be made more effective. In forty-one years of teaching I have never had any principal or superintendent suggest how could improve my teaching effectiveness. One principal observed a fifth grade spelling test and asked to see the papers when corrected. I handed him the alphabetically arranged papers according the children's last names. It was easier for me to place grades in my marking book. The principal asked me why the words were different on some of the papers. He had failed to understand I have given five different spelling tests to five different groups. The principal, though a pleasant individual, had never taught spelling, reading, language arts, or penmanship. He had been a mechanical engineer.

At another time, I remember attending a board of education meeting and a taxpayer asked the curriculum coordinator about a subject her child was taking in the eighth grade. The coordinator was unfamiliar with the subject and had to look in his briefcase to try and find the appropriate answer. Can you imagine working in private industry, receiving a salary of more than $80,000 and someone asks a question about your responsibility and you have no clue as to what the question is all about?

The novice teacher should be idealistic but at the same time leave a little room for reality. Do the best job you can and be honest with yourself and the children placed in your care. Your contemporaries are moved by strange powers. Some have selfish motives, ambitious motives, and God only knows how many other kind of motives.

We find the "do-gooders" raising money, then dictating how the money raised should be spent. This teacher remembers one mother demanding the sum of money raised be used immediately so her child would benefit from the purchase of library books.

Others demand a greater voice in school policy, the curricula, and special treatment for their child in school programs. Another mother wanted her child to play solo in the school concert because she was on the band committee.

The new teacher will be amazed, perhaps stunned by parental pressures. These are only possible because school administrators encourage parental involvement with improper guidelines. Once again, Dr. Joseph Priestly was right on the money. In essence, he believed the job of operating a school rests with the administration and staff. They are the experts. Parents are useful in passing the school budget and general suggestions. If the administrators are ineffective, then the representatives of the community, the board of education trustees, should replace the administrators. Here, we have the wagon again pulling the horses.

Parents have a selfish and understandable interest. That interest focuses on their children. If they contribute, they expect a return or dividend. It was the misfortune of one administrator to encourage unguided parental involvement. It became a typical case of the benefactor being gobbled up by the parents. He lost his job primarily because he was unable to satisfy many divergent parental demands.

HANDWRITING

Teachers handle children's papers daily. Reverend Norman Werling, a world famous handwriting expert, was invited to speak before our local association's faculty meeting. He told us graphology is a science of analyzing handwriting. His lecture was very informative. Basically, handwriting analysis can reveal a person's emotional condition and other negative traits as well as intelligence, will power, mental development, integrity, temperament, frustration, sociability, and aptitudes. Father Werling's system is a professional Gestalt analysis reduced to forty graphic features he rates on a seven-point continuum. Being able to identify children according to the four (Hippocrates and Galen) temperaments of melancholic, phlegmatic, choleric, and sanguine would favor a positive learning climate.

No doubt, graphoanalysis and graphology will be an important part of a future teacher's tools and should definitely be part of the teacher's curriculum at college. With proper training, all teachers will be able to identify and refer emotionally disturbed children.

FEBRUARY

Field Trips, Ideas

THE SHORTEST MONTH

In New Jersey, our shortest school month is February. Many school districts combine Washington and Lincoln's birthdays into a one-week vacation. We normally see our children less than fifteen school days. Many school districts also finalize field trips in the month of February.

FIELD TRIPS

Taking a school bus load of children to another location has been suggested by more than a several administrators, to be a vital educational experience. This teacher remembers, as a child, being taken through a Coca Cola plant and receiving a free bottle of soda and a pencil. It was exciting, but thinking back, it had little educational value. Some may say there may have been some value in watching the mass producing bottle machine pump out many bottles per minute. Others may logically support the social aspect of traveling outside the ghetto to a strange place with a familiar name

During the four decades of teaching, children often complain of visiting the same museum many times over. It happens often from kindergarten through the eighth grade. Many teachers moan of having to take children on a distant bus ride. Very rarely does a principal offer guidance in recommending a particular eventful experience as a possible curriculum tie-in. I have never heard of a principal going with a class on a field trip, let alone a superintendent.

If you work near a metropolis, you will have a tremendous opportunity to offer your children an enriching field trip experience. A novice teacher should prepare the class for the trip and have a meaningful follow-up activity. For example, one social studies field trip tied in the history of vessels crossing the Atlantic Ocean. We began with the Spanish looting the New World then moved on to the English immigrants and sailors not being able to bathe while confined in the tight quarters of the small ships. We discussed the rodent problem of eating and the contamination of food during those voyages. This was a major factor of many vessels failing to complete their missions to or from the New World. With the follow-up unit of studying coal and oil steamers both lessons worked well together. Our math lessons tried to solve problems related to ship tonnage, its length, capacity, and other statistical information drawn from the vessels the early explorers set sail on. We compared those facts with contemporary times. Research projects of gathering pictures and checking the daily New York Times shipping schedules of both arriving and departing times of ocean vessels from the New York harbor broaden the class interest.

Our planned field trip was to board the S.S. United States. It was our good fortune to have two warships berth in the same pier area. I asked a naval officer and received permission to board both vessels with my class. We first toured the ocean liner, then the light cruiser Southampton and the submarine Seawolf.

The return bus trip passed the west-side piers in New York City. We saw familiar names of ocean vessels we had read about and recorded from the New York Times newspaper.

Another interesting field trip, several years later, took us down to the Fulton Fish Market on the lower eastside of Manhattan. Our class saw an authentic Viking ship and boarded two 1900 era steamers.

Still another trip tied in the variety of people populating our metropolis with the huge skyscrapers in midtown New York. With a few telephone calls we visited Chinatown museum as well as traveling up to the top of the Twin Tower skyscraper. The class saw helicopters flying below the observation deck of this building. We viewed New York and New Jersey. The children also saw the Statue of Liberty. Our bus ride back to school detoured through the Black, Italian, Spanish, Jewish, German, and Hispanic neighborhoods. The most difficult part of any field trip, once underway, is finding bathroom facilities. Be sure to remind all your children to go to the bathroom before boarding the school bus.

In Chinatown, we had a bathroom emergency. Our bus driver stopped at Pace College for a bathroom emergency stop, without a minute to spare!

One reading lesson focused on the life of Carl Akeley, the world famous naturalist and hunter. He is credited with advancing the science of taxidermy. Since class interest was very high and my knowledge of hunting and taxidermy very limited, I checked the yellow pages of the telephone book. In our county was listed a master taxidermist. We found he had a sizable workshop. A telephone call led to a class trip to his professional workshop and mountings. The experience was educational and worthwhile for both the class and teacher. One student asked, "You said almost anything can be cleansed and mounted. Can you stuff or mount a human being?" Mr. Moran, the kind and patient taxidermist, smiled and nodded, "Yes."

A visit to the New York Times or your county/state newspaper office building is an interesting tour that may supplement your language arts curriculum.

The Audubon Society and county parks are also good sources of flora and fauna related experiences for an educational field trip.

A field trip to West Point is an excellent tie-in with American history. We visited the museum and walked through the cemetery. The class made several charcoal rubbings of the names of generals from their tombstones.

Another year we did some charcoal rubbings in the Trinity Church cemetery on Wall Street, in New York City. Our children obtained the rubbings of Watts and Alexander Hamilton, among others.

With language arts, another class trip visited the offices of United Press International and the Associated Press news services in midtown Manhattan. While in New York we toured the NBC building and heard our school's name mentioned over a radio station. Before boarding the school bus we walked into Saint Patrick's Cathedral. Inside the cathedral we saw statues and paintings of bishops, archbishops, and cardinals. We viewed the skullcaps of the dead cardinals nailed to the high ceiling of the cathedral.

The next day a child asked me what my religion is. I told the young man I believe in all religions that honor and respect their fellow human beings. He gave me a Star of David medal I wore all year. Good thing! Every once in a while, the child would ask to see the medal.

If you are unfamiliar with your particular school area, usually the school office secretary or media specialist (librarian), has a compilation of field trips previously taken by other teachers. Another source could be some person in central administration whose responsibility is to order the transportation necessary for field trips. Try to tie-in the most difficult or most curious curriculum unit to a planned field trip. It is a wise practice to telephone a person at your field trip destination several weeks before leaving school. This will confirm all arrangements.

ASSEMBLIES

What seems to be difficult for both educators and parents to understand is the teaching day has a limited number of hours, usually five. The more subjects or gimmicks we insert into that time span the less time we have to teach subjects of learning or core curriculum disciplines.

The school year usually begins with an introductory band assembly program. A musician from a supplying music company demonstrates as well as explains ten to fifteen musical instruments. The music teacher then has permission forms duplicated and distributed to every child in the assembly.

In October, your school will have a Halloween Class Play, or have some visiting drama group come for another assembly.

Schools also have the police or fire officials address all children at another assembly.

In November, an assembly is scheduled with children listening to the school band, chorus, and chorale.

December hits a high with the band's holiday concert that includes class skits and a chorus singing Christmas and Hanukkah carols. The day before the Christmas holiday vacation break, band members with blaring instruments, flood the school'' corridors.

January has been the month of an assembly for folk music groups and a Martin Luther King Day commemoration ceremony.

The shortest month, February, usually has an assembly with someone from the Franklin Institute. Some other theatrical song and dance group also comes in to amuse our children.

An assembly of colonial life welcomes the month of March. Several weeks later we usually have one or two class-plays.

The two assemblies in April may include the school band's Spring Concert, as well as another visiting minstrel show. Class plays are sometimes also added to the festivities.

In May, your school may have a performance of Sorcerer's Apprentice and the Legend of Sleepy Hollow. Experience at the secondary level included a three-day Shakespeare Festival. This included nearby high schools visiting and contributing their performers. This disrupts not only the regular learning day of many involved students but spreads to the entire school population. The "Bard" dialogue is often contemporary slang and the performers resemble burlesque skits.

The June finale includes an athletic and scholastic awards assembly. Field Day ribbons, attendance certificates, and other rewards are then distributed.

The novice teacher may ask, "What other events happen that will add to the reduction of learning time?"

Remembering all schools are not the same, some other events may include a Fun Fair Poster Drawing Contest, a visit by your local dentist, an assembly to show the students photographs of themselves taken by members of the student council or others. Perhaps a book fair displayed in the gymnasium or auditorium. Popular gimmicks and time wasters are: School's newspaper and Year Book assemblies, Freedom Day, Crazy Hat Day, Dress up and Dress Down days, Standardized Test Days, Health film for girls assembly, Half-Day sessions for parent conferences; students from the elementary school visiting the high school; chorale and band members visiting International Business Machine or some other corporation for a song festival. We had the school band and chorus, perform during school hours, at a new store opening. Other time wasters include Field Day Contests, Outdoor Nature events, school breakfast get-togethers socials at each grade level, and at different times. And the beat goes on.

The beginning teacher may ask, "How much time does a student lose from actual classroom learning?"

My personal accounting figures, given to the board of education, was accumulated one frustrating year. The tally indicated an average of twelve school days, per pupil or sixty hours of learning was lost. This figure does not include sick days or excused absences. That amount of class time lost is tragic. It can never be replaced. Financially, the low cost estimate was figured to be $750,000. This figure includes the paid salaries of teachers, maintenance and office personnel, and the expense of visiting performers.

The more liberal the policy of your school system is relating to assemblies, school band, and other nonsensical frivolities, the greater loss of teaching time and children working on the sequential building blocks of learning. A very important question to ask, "How can we measure the continuity of learning lost by constant interruptions?" The truthful answer should be, "We can't and neither can anyone else."

Another question suggested, "How much time is lost trying to bring the proper learning climate back to where it was before an energetic assembly musical event?" Personal experience has correlated the recovery time of an athlete after a strenuous exercise or competitive event. What would you guess a student's mental recovery time would be from a rock or contemporary music assembly? There have been some assemblies that excite a student the entire school day. Problems from that event have carried over to conflicts on the school bus, lunchroom, and parking lot.

When students return to class, the teacher needs an adjustment time trying to refocus twenty-five, hyper-kinetic students. Lunch is usually scheduled at the midpoint of the school day. Many schools have morning (AM) assemblies that begin at the start of the school day. There are Mid AM assemblies scheduled to begin about one hour into the school day. Then we have (PM) assemblies that begin about one hour before the students leave school for the day. With an assembly or some senseless interruption, the students don't lose one hour. The time lost is at least half a school day. The educated guess is two and a half-hours. This time is calculated from the time lost by the assembly plus recovery time.

IDEAS

The key to any idea is the value it has as it relates to something being taught in the classroom. Find out if your community has a civil defense transmitter and receiver as a left over from World War II or any of the other wars. Perhaps someone in your community is a "ham operator." If the electronic equipment is usable, your children could converse with other children from another state or country. A great social studies supplement concerned with customs, habits, food, government, and other related topics could add a new dimension to your class unit.

If your school is located in a rural or suburban district, check out the state university's agricultural department for assistance to further or develop a school science area of farm and forestry study. It could replace the wasted time students spend in study halls eating, drinking, and talking.

If your school does not have a spelling bee contest, why not create one? Begin at your school, and then later challenge a neighboring school. Ask a local merchant to donate a small prize for the winner(s). McDonalds, Burger King, Wendy's and a few others have been very generous.

Ask your children if their parents have an interesting job or hobby. This teacher had a parent who tapped sugar maple trees. He became an integral part of the class work dealing with Indians and maple syrup.

Invite a handwriting expert in to speak at a teachers' faculty meeting. Be sure to receive your principal's approval. If the interest is there, explore the possibility of having an "after school" class of teachers being instructed by the expert. It will be a valuable tool for teachers to identify possible student emotional problems.

Propose a teacher exchange program with a nearby school. Try to gain the support of your superintendent and principal. The purpose is to infuse new ideas on methods and techniques of teaching various subjects. Suggest a one or two week exchange with perhaps one or two teachers. Develop the plan from this meager beginning.

Invite talented or gifted people to your teachers' faculty meetings to spark teaching resources and learning. The guest could be a writer, horticulturist, an artist, or any main interest areas suggested by faculty members.

A novice teacher may propose a county, elementary grade level, contest in any subject area or any specific event.

With all that said, this veteran teacher would like to inject a word of caution. The beginning teacher is energetic and full of enthusiasm and is oftentimes a threat to a veteran, or perhaps a "burned out" teacher. Whatever proposal the new teacher may embark upon, it should be done with that sensitivity in mind. Utilizing fellow colleagues' suggestions and opinions should be welcomed and that doesn't mean surrendering your own plans. Being tactful is the key to your future success.

MARCH

Background, C.T.B.S., Associations

BACKGROUND

Within the last decade, New Jersey has been striving to improve the quality of education statewide. This involves more than 600 school districts. Since 1664, the days of Lord Berkeley and Sir George Carteret, education has been left in the hands of local citizens. A state wide assessment test uncovered vast areas of student academic deficiencies.

The New Jersey Assessment Tests measures children in four different grade levels. It is encouraging to note some improvement. This improvement has been attributed to both increased parental concern and pressures brought upon the administrative staffs of all school districts. The school personnel have eliminated or carefully screened many pilot programs lacking the validity of time. In some cases, a tightening up of discipline and student absenteeism has improved the classroom environment.

Discipline, however, is only a small part of delivering a quality education. Many are amazed and have professionally admired the neat and orderly operations of private and parochial schools. Though less costly to operate, these schools have had notable success primarily due to discipline. If we were to compare the quality of the educational expertise of both groups of teachers, the qualifications of public school teachers far exceed their fellow contemporaries. A comparison of the National Merit Scholarship winners and the Scholastic Aptitude Test scores arrived at on a ratio of school population is a determining factor. Unfortunately, the public schools have separate philosophies, different textbooks, revolving-door superintendents, and have remained entities onto themselves.

New Jersey still has a long way to go to truly improve her national ranking of being 46th out of our 50 states. She has consistently hired education commissioners from outside the state just as local school districts do when seeking a superintendent or principal. Not only are most commissioners unfamiliar with our statewide problems but many never taught school. This teacher spoke to the Assistant Commissioner of Education, in New Jersey, several years ago. We met at a luncheon in Trenton. He was in favor of mainstreaming mentally disturbed children with the normal school enrollment. He thought it would be a good idea to have retarded and disturbed children in the same class with all other children. I asked him if he ever taught in that kind of environment. His reply was, "No. I am a psychologist." That figures. He was unaware of a teacher's responsibility to teach and extend all children. With a range extending from the retarded to the gifted, the teacher's task is impossible. If we break down a class into four or five ability groups in each subject, then we need four or five lesson plans for each subject. If a teacher taught spelling, arithmetic, science, health, reading, language arts, social studies, and penmanship. It would be unrealistic to believe a teacher will spend five or more hours each week preparing forty lesson plans. It is also unrealistic to believe that same teacher will spend even more time correcting weekly test papers from so many different groups.

This veteran teacher was greatly amused when reading about the New Jersey Commissioner of Education, Fred Burke, visiting a high school class. He went to the chalkboard and wrote five words. Three of the five words were misspelled. He too, was never a teacher.

CALIFORNIA TEST OF BASIC SKILLS

In mid-March, four school days are set aside for children taking the California Test of Basic Skills or C.T.B.S. tests. Children are tested in reading, math, science, social studies, and reference skills. The results are usually published in mid-June of the same year. There is a yearly comparison made of every child's past and present scores. For the novice teacher, it may be a nerve-racking experience. The results may have you thinking, "Have I done an adequate job?" At this point in time, it is really too late to worry. A concert pianist worries about performing in a recital at least six months beforehand. If he has practiced the many hours he should have, the results are predictable. My favorite pianist, Alicia De Larrocha, when flying across the Atlantic for a European performance, practices on a cardboard keyboard utilizing the hours spent in flight. The same discipline is necessary for an athlete. Practice is the constant necessary for the desired result. An optimum effort is required for the maximum result.

This teacher has never worried about any standardized tests because each and every day's teaching effort was the best possible. Perusing past test results and most often incorrect answered questions, focuses on areas that should be stressed a little more than most other areas. It also helped me improve by having supplementary material to aid those areas that give my children the most difficulty. The novice teacher should always keep in mind poor results are also the responsibility of the administration permitting numerous meaningless assemblies accompanied by many other nonsensical frivolities.

What has always disturbed this teacher is the fact schools spend tens of thousands of dollars for the C.T.B.S. tests and failed to make better use of the information gathered. There are two write or printouts for each child tested. One contains the composite scores while the other has a breakdown of all questions answered correctly denoted with a plus (+) sign. Questions missed have a minus (-) sign. It would be a great benefit to a teacher to know at the beginning of a school year, the major areas of difficulty, in each subject tested, for each child, in each class. It would also be a great benefit if the computer told every teacher what pages, in each textbook, should be stressed and re-enforced for each child. It would be of great significance if every principal supplemented major areas of concern with both material and gifted individuals in those particular areas infused into the school's learning processes.

Going one step further, we could also have a write-out for parents telling them of supplementary materials that would be most beneficial for their child. This would have a great impact especially during the vacation months of July and August.

I favor regents core curriculum tests. The negative criticism often heard is, "Teachers will be teaching for the regents." That's great! We can be sure our children will be at least fortunate enough to get that amount of instruction. It was painful to read Edward Singletary, of the District of Columbia's, "Financial Responsibility and Management Assistance Authority." He states, "When only 22 percent of fourth graders are reading at grade level, we've got to do something and if it means taking away home rule temporarily in this one area, I am not disturbed by that."

TEACHER ASSOCIATIONS

In most cases the novice teacher will have an opportunity to join four teacher groups. There will be the local, county, state, and national associations. No longer may anyone select less than four. In New Jersey, our choice is to join all four or none at all.

Your local association will have its own constitution to negotiate teacher-board of education contracts. Most local groups also have the secretarial and maintenance affiliations as part of their association. A breakdown of committees are negotiations, salary and teacher benefits, human relations, professional rights and responsibilities, professional relations, student relations, secretarial, custodial, instructional and professional development, followed by governmental relations and citizenship.

There is no better way to become part of your new school than to join a committee and have some input to develop a professional relationship with your colleagues. Common sense dictates it would be wiser to have tenure before working on the negotiations and salary committees. If you insist on being a vocal part of those committees, do a great deal of listening. Take notes during the exchange of dialogue of your committee and that of the trustees. When the committees have periodic breaks for coffee or private meetings, interject your comments to your chairperson.

This teacher has been a member of the negotiations committee several times spending more hours in this stimulating arena of arbitration. Tempers flare and harsh words are exchanged. When all is said and done there is a close bond of camaraderie established as well as a fall-out of unfortunate victims.

An important feature of our local association, besides all the benefits negotiated, is the grievance procedure it has developed. We have four levels in our contract. At Level I the teacher discussing a problem with the principal. If that fails to resolve the problem in a given time limit, the teacher moves on to Level II. The meeting here is with the superintendent with the same format. If unresolved we move on to Level III and a meeting with the board of education. If the problem remains unresolved, Level IV is the final step. The grievance is submitted to arbitration under the Voluntary Labor Arbitration Rules of the American Arbitration Association within thirty days of receipt of the Board's decision. A teacher filing is supported by the grievance chairman as well as a representative from the state association.

The county association is more distant and its function is trying to keep districts, within the county, aware of events beneficial to all. The county association sponsors teacher workshops, offers advice, and gives cards for shopping discounts. It has an annual dinner. The dinner has a prominent state or federal official invited as a guest speaker.

The New Jersey Education Association is a well-run organization with a corporate-like staff. Our state is divided into sixteen regions with each having its own UniServ Field representative and business office. We also have six other areas. These are communications, government relations, instruction, research, business, and an intern foundation. A monthly magazine and newspaper keeps all members informed of mutual professional concerns. The annual teachers' convention is held in Atlantic City in mid-November. This teacher has found the state association extremely helpful and supportive in countless areas of personal concern and need. Among the many benefits we derive from our fantastic state association is the legal protection offered. An attorney is provided and paid for by the state association. Without reservation, this forty-one year professional teacher would strongly advise the novice teacher to become a unified member and hopefully take an active part in whatever state committee you may be so interested in.

On a personal level, several years ago, this teacher became a state committee member for the exceptional children. Three years experience was both fruitful and frustrating. It was worthwhile supporting and seeing our governor sign bill S-3067. This bill was the source of obtaining state aid for handicapped students in the resource room program. It was frustrating because most members on the committee either weren't interested or lacked the background experience acknowledging the need for county schools for our gifted and talented children. The proposal, if accepted, would have been a giant leap for upgrading all schools. Perhaps my dream was unrealistic at that time and place. The major thrust of this committee was for the mentally retarded. Why the committee had both the mentally retarded and the gifted/talented under the same umbrella remains a mystery.

Some time ago, in annoyance, this teacher went to see a member in the Bergen County Freeholders office seeking advice. She was a brilliant woman who had a retarded son and was unhappy with what the schools were doing for her child. Two decades prior to her nomination as a freeholder, she decided to become involved with local politics. In a short period of time she ran and won a seat she currently occupied. Once elected, she became the chairperson of state aid funneling down for the county education programs. Our county freeholder skillfully directed her energies to directing state monies toward programs and schools aiding her retarded son and everyone else needing that specialized assistance. Today, thanks to this lovely, extremely bright mother, we have sixteen schools and programs aiding handicapped children. Her greatest contribution to society will not be found in the very popular books she's noted for but rather for the permanent schools and thousands of children that have survived because of her efforts.

New Jersey does not have one school similar to Stuyvesant High School or the LaGuardia School of Music and Arts located in New York City. Five to ten percent of our children who are gifted and talented, are the most handicapped in New Jersey. If the novice teacher, admires the Hunter College Elementary School, the Bronx High School of Science, or the already two schools mentioned, don't waste your time on local or state committees. Even the local politicians can't help. Been there, done that! Become involved with local politics with an eye on the County Board of Freeholders. Republicans seem to always win in Bergen County. Become a Republican and get elected. Be sure to play down your primary goal since it affects, as a State Senator frankly told me, only ten percent of the voters and you need fifty-one percent to win the election. Listen to the usual political rhetoric and drivel, smile, and shake as many hands as possible. Once elected, your goal is the same as the example previously given. Then and only then, will the scales of justice be affected. The thousands of students traveling to the New York City schools from New Jersey will come back home.

The State Senator was a good listener giving very practical advice. He was told of what affect the discovery or invention of one person could have on everyone and only the gifted have that ability to make it happen. The official was told of how the retarded affect their family. The average person affects immediate family members and a slightly wider ripple of outsiders. The gifted has and can affect everyone. They always have and always will.

If the task is too large an order, the suggestion to parents is to carefully select your child's teachers. Investigate the teachers available in each succeeding grade. If you find this difficult, a parent always has the option to run for the board of education. Almost all of the more than 300 board of education trustees I've known in 41 years have had children in school. Experience indicates many administrators and trustees prefer non-confrontational taxpayers and parents. If this is too radical a measure for you to consider, remember a school year lost is one that can never be replaced. Success, as well as failure, has a beginning. With more than 37,000 children taught, this teacher has seen the results of both involved parents and those who let "nature take its course."

The fourth association we have is the National Education Association. It is headquartered in Washington, D.C. It is far-removed from most of those teaching, but has our interest at heart. The N.E.A. is a liberal lobbying entity, offering benefits. We are kept abreast of national issues by receiving a monthly magazine as well as a newspaper supplement.

On May 19, 1997 in the New York Post, the headline read, "Public School Teachers Union Gives Itself Failing Report Card." The article reported, "With 2.2 million members, the N.E.A. must do a complete about-face, shifting its approach from that of an industrial union to one that embraces attributes of craft unionism, in which ensuring quality workers is just as important as raising wages and benefits at the bargaining table. Failure to change means further marginalization and possible organizational death."

Interestingly, the article concluded, "The N.E.A. can best serve its members and public school children by reducing its top heavy staff, advocating merit pay for teachers, decreasing its political activism, and supporting strong charter school legislation."

APRIL

Class Plays

CLASS PLAYS

April is a month that has many interruptions. We have the Easter vacation, Field Day, half-day sessions, chorale trips to shopping malls and International Business Machines Office musicals. A dentist visits our school at an assembly, the school nurse decides to check the hearing of all children, she also checks the curvature of the spine, we have a school band Spring Concert, and several class-plays.

Why April some may asked? I've asked myself that question every year for forty years. The most probable answer may have something to do with Spring, April showers, and the emerging from the doldrums of the long, cold winter. That's an educated guess. No pun intended!

Let's explore several ways a novice teacher can find, develop, and have children deliver a positive theatrical performance. Initially, the teacher should have some idea as to the subject matter of the play. Do you want it to extend the Greek Mythology chapter in both the reading and language arts textbook?

Do you feel your children would best benefit from a play exploring the mysteries of astronomy?

We had a field trip to the Hayden Planetarium in New York City. This was the catalyst for a play about Galileo. The class made paper constructed planets. They were hung from the entrance to the auditorium ceiling to the rear of the stage or some seventy-five feet.

Social studies can be a very popular source for play material. With the many interesting people of the past, the selection is limitless. The media center or library has magazines with play scripts at suggested grade levels. If you want to try and produce a video-play, look around your town or city for ready-made props. For instance, one year my fifth grade class video-taped, "The Battle of Bull Run." We utilized the town's historical train and railroad depot. In a short distance from the depot is a wooden, walk bridge and a small pond. Our second scene was shot in the nearby county park that contained an aged, leaning barn. The children made a huge sign, "Centerville." It was attached to the side of the barn. At the railroad depot, our huge sign, "Manassas Junction" covered the name of our town.

Once a subject area has been decided upon, an effort is made to accumulate background information. Both the teacher and class then develop the script. Some teachers, striving for perfection, hesitate to have their children work on the script. Children are not professional writers, and no one expects a Hollywood production. The novice teacher will find the more children become involved in a project, the more exciting it becomes for them. Most importantly, the development of an original script requires answers to many questions. The creative atmosphere in this situation is very rewarding for everyone and a great deal of fun.

Being more specific, this teacher begins by dividing the class into four groups. Carefully place your class leaders evenly within those groups. One method is to have them stand in front of the classroom or have one leader stand in each corner of the classroom. From that position, each leader selects someone from the class. The teacher records each selection and the name or number of each group. Each group is given a particular assignment. When we wrote the script on the life of Thomas Edison, a group was assigned to write about our greatest genius from birth to age twenty-one. The second group investigated his age from twenty-two through forty-two. The third group was assigned his age from forty-three through sixty-three. The last group had Thomas Alva from age sixty-four until he expired at the ripe old age of eighty-four. Each child was a character in the play. They also painted scenery or helped on the stage. Our media specialist or librarian was of great help delineating the highlights of Edison for each group. For scenery we used paper from a huge roll obtained from the school office supply room sanctuary. The roll measured one yard wide. We had three sheets approximately fifteen feet long and three yards wide. With masking tape and glue the children made three wide strips. They outlined the scenes in pencil and later used watercolor. At the end of the period, the work was stapled to the side and front chalkboards of the classroom. It is time-consuming and the children worked in late afternoons. Several after-school sessions were needed to complete the work on time.

On the day of the performance, we carefully carried all scenes to the stage and attached them to wooden supports. Between scenes we removed one page from the wooden supports and re-arranged the stage furniture. The teacher's role was trying not to watch or become excited in the event of forgotten lines during the class performance or scenery collapsing. When a child slammed a door, everything on stage seemed to wobble. A teacher's overall calm manner has a stable affect on the children's panic feelings or stage fright. A forgotten line or word is not a tragedy but a valuable and memorable experience for the student. Giving a play requires a great deal of patience and homework. Accomplishment and a shared experience unites all members of your class with one another and with their teacher.

In my first year of teaching we had a play dealing with health. About half way through the play, fifth grade boy either forgot his lines or was so nervous he repeated a line said at the beginning of the play. Sure enough the response was as it had been and the play became a replay. Seems only a few teachers realized what had happened and we all had a great laugh when it was over.

Several teachers asked for some help after we created our own video-tape. With the "Battle of Bull Run" the script was dissected. The media specialist gave me several books to read. The battle was broken down into the following shooting scenes, after the video camera zoomed in on our huge thirty by four foot sign reading, "Battle of Bull Run, July 21, 1861."

SCENE 1:   **Confederates mass at Manassas Junction Camera close-up on Rebels singing, "The Bonnie Blue Flag," and "Eatin' Goober Peas."**

SCENE 2:   **General McDowell's (Union) army marches from Centerville towards Manassas Junction singing, "Battle Hymn of the Republic," "John**

Brown's Body," and "Tenting on the Old Camp Ground."

SCENE 3:   General Johnston (Conf.) moves from Shenandoah Valley to Manassas
             Via the railroad. (a first time in warfare.)

SCENE 4:   The Union attacks their foes left flank at the wooden bridge. General
             Evans (Conf.) is driven back.

SCENE 5:   General Evans (Conf.) sends message to Generals Johnston and
             Beauregard. He drops back north of Warrenton Turnpike.

SCENE 6:   On Henry House Hill, Gen. Beauregard (Conf.) sets up a new line
             To stop Gen. McDowell (Union).

SCENE 7:   Gen. Evans(Union) men run wile Gen.Bee (Conf.) sees and announces,
             "General Jackson's(Conf.) men hold the line like a stonewall!"

SCENE 8:   (Artificial smoke). The Battle. Gen. Jackson's brigade holds the line.
             The Union pushes the left flank.

SCENE 9:   RR train arrives with Gen. Johnston's troops commanded by Gen.

Kirby-Smith(Conf.) He immediately joins the battle and strikes the Union's right flank.

SCENE 10:   Gen. McDowell's(Union) tired men panic and run.

SCENE 11:   Confederates cheer and sing, "Dixie." The South or Confederates won The first major battle of the Civil War.

With the above outline, a list was made of the major characters including a narrator. The cast consisted of Confederate Generals Bee, Beauregard, Stonewall Jackson, Kirby-Smith, Evans, and Johnston. The Union Generals were McDowell and Patterson.

It is difficult for most people to envision a whole battle. The battle scenes were dissected into three major areas. All children received Xeroxed copies of the three major areas. The first showed Bull Run Stream running diagonally across the paper. The upper right hand corner had McDowell's army advancing on Warrenton Turnpike towards the middle of the left side of the paper. On the lower third of the paper this teacher drew railroad road tracks and a large dot indicating the town of Manassas Junction. Completing this first map were two dashes about one-half inch each pointing down from the upper right hand corner indicating the second army of McDowell advancing about eighty degrees from the first army.

The second Xeroxed map had the same outline as the first except the armies have further advanced. McDowell's first army continues down the turnpike and crosses over Bull Run Stream with his main attack. He is met by the Confederates at Henry

House Hill. McDowell's army, commanded by General Patterson, panics and runs. Confederate General Bee shouts and immortalizes his comrade, General Jackson, with, "He's standing like a stonewall!" The second Union army pushes the Confederates left flank.

The third Xeroxed map advances from the first two by showing a dotted line from the railroad station at Manassas Junction and General Kirby-Smith's (Conf.) joining the battle and turning the tide from possible defeat to victory!

At this point you have the plot and overview of the story of your video play. Now you need the vehicle in which to tell your story. On a blank master Xerox measuring eight and one half by fourteen inches, type or print on the long side. Divide the long side into columns and breakdown each element of the major points into: SHOT, SCENE, ACTION, CAMERA, SOUND/DIALOGUE, AND TIME. Your script should look something like this:

SHOT 1; SCENE Name/Child; ACTION Introduction; CAMERA Full View; SOUND/DIALOGUE "The date...July 21, 1861...." TIME (for this SHOT) 2 minutes.

SHOT 2; SCENE (Second child); ACTION Child near a large map; CAMERA Full View; SOUND/DIALOGUE Child points out highlights of the map and opposing armies and generals; TIME 3 minutes.

SHOT 3; SCENE Rear car of a train; ACTION Confederates singing "Goober Peas"; CAMERA Pans all soldiers SOUND/DIALOGUE Confederate songs; TIME 5 minutes

The first shot was taken at the historical railroad depot in town. The children painted a huge sign, "Manassas Junction." We hung the sign over the town's signpost. Our second shot was at the same location but slightly to the right of the narrator of the first shot. This second scene had a different student explaining the three large maps in detail. The maps were enlarged and colored for the camera viewing. Blue depicted the Union Armies while red was the designated color of the Confederates. The narrator had a long, pointed dowel and her assistant turned the sheets.

The third shot was at the same general location but viewed from the rear of the depot. We had children sitting on the steps of the train's entrance and also around the entrance to the station house.

After shooting our scenes at Manassas Junction, the next time we video taped, we traveled about a mile from the school to the county park. With the same size sign used at the railroad station, the children painted another sign, "Centerville." This time the scene was General McDowell's Union army. The dialogue of the soldiers centered about "Jonny Reb." It closes out with the soldiers all singing, "The Battle Hymn of the Republic."

In our battle scenes we used dry ice in water for smoke. The children also had flour stuffed into toy rifles. Mothers provided the uniforms for all the soldiers. At a signal the children blew into the barrel of their rifle to give the impression of gunfire. The cameraman was careful just to show the smoke coming out of the rifle. Dubbed in sound effects included the train whistle and the locomotive engine running, cannons exploding and rifle firings.

When the film was completed, the media center cameraman replaced a bugle retreat sound given very earnestly by a small fifth grade boy. The "bugle retreat scene" was dubbed in by a musician from a classical symphony orchestra. When the children viewed the tape and that particular scene, a thunder of laughter exploded. It became one highlight of the school year.

The experience supplemented our textbook by research of both the children and myself. At this battle we discovered crowds of picnickers traveled south from Washington,D.C. to Centerville, Virginia. They came by horseback and carriage as if going to the Super Bowl. As spectators, they wanted to watch General McDowell's army sweep aside the Confederates. Instead, we learned, they found themselves entangled with the Union's retreating soldiers.

This new experience of using the video camera was later shared with other teachers. We listed the eight major battles or events of the Civil War. These were the First Battle of Bull Run, Battle of Antietam, Gettysburg, Battle of Vicksburg, Battle of Lookout Mountain, Battle of the Wilderness, Sherman's March Through Georgia, and Lee's Surrender.

Our class video play was exhibited at the local shopping mall that had contributions from most schools in our county. More importantly, it was an effective learning lesson.

CHART #1 BATTLE OF BULL RUN
(3) MAJOR AREAS FOR FILMING

Shooting Scene #1
(Distribute a Xerox copy of this battle to the whole class)

McDowell's 1st Army- Led by General Patterson

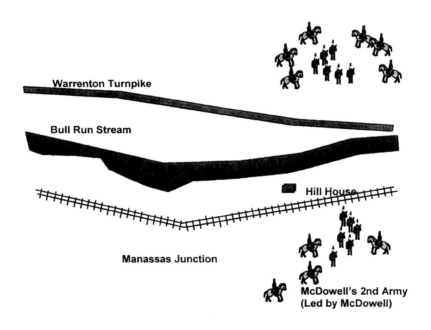

CHART #2　　BATTLE　OF　BULL　RUN

Shooting Scene #2

Same outline as Chart #1 except the armies advance further. General Patterson's Union army and Confederates clash at Henry House Hill. The Union army panics and runs. Confederate General Bee shouts, and immortalizes his comrade, General Jackson with, "He's standing like a stonewall!"

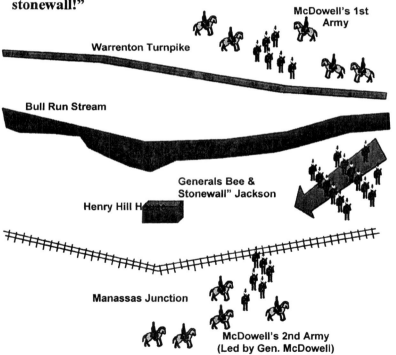

CHART #3 BATTLE OF BULL RUN
Shooting Scene #3

The battle advances showing Confederate General Kirby-Smith's army joining the battle and turning the tide from defeat to victory.

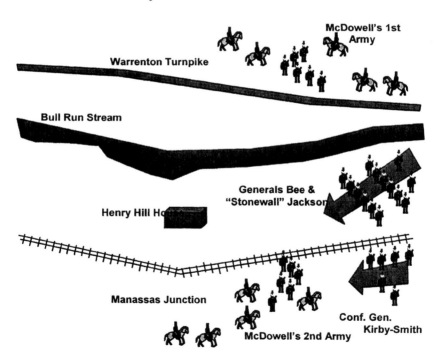

CHART #4 BATTLE OF BULL RUN
SCRIPT

SHOT 1; SCENE Narrator; **ACTION** Introduction
CAMERA Full View; **SOUND/DIALOGUE**

"The date is July 21, 1861. The place, Manassas Junction,
Virginia. The event, The first major battle of the Civil War.
The South or Confederacy was hoping for an early victory
and end to the war. About 6 miles northeast of here we find
the North or Union Armies, commanded by General
Dowell. As a connecting link between both armies runs Bull
Run Stream." Time: 4 minutes.

SHOT 2, SCENE 2nd Narrator; **ACTION** Near Map;
CAMERA Full View; **S/D** (Student explains Charts 2 & 3)
Time: 5 minutes.

SHOT 3, SCENE Last car of RR train. Confederate soldiers
Scattered on and near train. **ACTION** soldiers eating
Goober Peas. **CAMERA** scans and zeros in on several
soldiers. **S/D** Soldier #1 "Them tha Yankees over
Centerville are agettin' restless! I overheard them tha
captin assayin they're amovin to the old Henry Hill's
(pointing) House over yonder. He's done said the other
part of old McDowell's army is acomin' dead ahead of us!"
Soldier #2: "That's what I aheared too, Jeb. They're tryin'
to surround us! Must think we southern boys are out
apickin' magnolias!" Soldier #3: "Our General
Beauregard has them a all figgered out. He's acallin his ole

buddies General Smith and Johnston. They should be a-comin down these ole railroad tracks from down the Shenandoah. Yep! I done aheared it myself. (the soldier concluded, slapping himself on the side of his leg.) Soldier #1 "Hot Diggs! That'll give us nough to drive dem Yanks straight back to Washington!" They begin to sing "Eatin' Goober Peas" with everyone joining in. Time: 5 minutes

Several years later, my class had expressed a great interest in Greek mythology. Echo and Narcissus stirred up the most children's excitement of wanting to learn more about mythology. We followed the interest with filmstrips and tapes. The most favored by the class, in addition to Echo and Narcissus was Daphne and Apollo, Orpheus and Eurydice, (my favorite) Philemon and Baucis, followed by Perseus and Medusa, and naturally, The Trojan War. Using the same format as the Battle of Bull Run, we video taped all six myths. Every child loves to be on film.

The first recorded was Philemon and Baucis. The tale is a lovely myth stressing the morale of being kind to your neighbor. This leads to another very important aspect of every teacher's career goals. Young children are the essence to the continuation of a sane and healthy civilization. The ancient Spartans knew the importance of nurturing children. Thomas Jefferson certainly understood the importance of educating our children to further our republic. Adolph Hitler knew it and we know it. Everyone should be aware of always stressing things that are good and wholesome. It is the foundation of our beliefs. Why is it important to love and obey our father and mother? Why is it wrong to take something that belongs to someone else? Why is it bad to smoke, drink alcohol, and use drugs? In the case of Greek mythology, there is an underlying morale that stresses the good in mankind. In every play look for some significant theme or plot of the story. If your children learn nothing else but how to be good and how to love their neighbor, then your teaching career will be an overwhelming success. You have struck at the very heart of teaching. There is nothing more satisfying than to help mold a child's life.

GREEK MYTHOLOGY
"PHILEMON AND BAUCIS"

SHOT 1 SCENE: Zeus and Mercury; ACTION: they're talking; CAMERA Close-up S/D. Both looking at a pool of water. Background: water music.

SHOT 2 SCENE: Zeus and Mercury; ACTION: They're walking. Mercury points to a little shack. CAMERA: 10 feet; S/D: Mercury: "Let's see if anyone's home in this little house."

SHOT 3 SCENE: The Gods walk up to the door. ACTION: Zeus knocks on the door. CAMERA: 20 feet; S/D: The door opens. An old man smiles. "May I help you? My name is Philemon. May I help you?" He extends his hand. "Please enter my humble home and meet my wife, Baucis. (He holds his other hand out.) We have been married many years in this humble house."

SHOT 4 SCENE: Dinner; ACTION: You are welcome to join us for dinner. Philemon pours wine in four glasses while

Baucis serves food. CAMERA: 10 feet; S/D: Philemon keeps pouring wine that doesn't stop flowing. He exclaims, "The bottle was almost empty yet it keeps pouring wine!" Time: 3 minutes.

Most teachers seem to prefer the usual plays performed on the stage of the school's auditorium. Many colleagues have utilized such stories as Sindbad, Paul Revere, Rikki Ticki Tavi, Paul Bunyan, and Henry Hudson.

Another possibility for a beginning teacher is having a marionette play. The play we gave, several years ago was, "Beauty and the Beast." The characters needed were a merchant, his daughter, a juggler, an oriental dancer, the beast, a little dog (Kasha), Prince Abmed, and the wicked sisters, Queika and Fatima. The media center had a "How To" book about marionette making and how to build a stage. The high school wood shop teacher helped by assisting us cutting out the body parts from wood. The class used styrofoam, base-ball like spheres for the heads of our marionettes. A class father volunteered and built a wooden stage. Another child's mother made the stage curtains. After the marionettes were made, the child's parents had them clothed. The marionettes were strung and I taught our children how to manipulate the strings. We quickly realized reciting lines and manipulating strings became very difficult for the ten-year olds. Common sense had us record the dialogue and sound effects. All the children had to do was to coordinate listening to the dialogue with the movement of the marionettes. One major problem was children have a tendency to have their characters "fly" instead of working the strings and have them walk from one position on stage, to another. The key to achieving our goal was a great deal of practice.

After several performances in school we gave a Saturday performance for children in the primary schools. We then received permission to travel to Saint Joseph's Orphanage in our county. The experience was memorable. After the performance, the curtains opened and our students walked to the front of the stage with their marionettes. The children in the audience touched and tugged on the marionettes, lovingly. One little girl of five or six years, accidentally pulled down the pants of the Prince marionette. Suddenly, more than two hundred children became silent. A robust, jovial nun smiled and the good time resumed.

MAY

Projects, Re-evaluation

RE-EVALUATION

May is a month of five weeks. Teachers should be aware of the limited time remaining of the school year. The month of May is the time to re-appraise where your class is, academically, and what your remaining teaching goals should be. Some veteran teachers revise their long-term lesson plans and fine tune weekly plans during this month. If you are one of the few on schedule, perhaps other supplementary ideas and program enrichments could be inserted into your plans. Now is the time to readjust your time schedule. As your class work finalizes, you may want to spend more time with activities that extend almost completed subject areas.

CLASS PROJECTS

Plaster of Paris molds have always been a simple, yet interesting project activity. For those children who like making molds, a suggestion would be to inform parents to escort their children to the local hardware store when purchasing the plaster. The whip cream mixture is poured into molds and left in school, overnight, to harden. The molds can directly relate to class subject matter. We have had Indian molds, flowers, animals, historical American political figures, birds, and other related subjects. We have also extended the pouring of molds to animal tracks found outdoors. Children have also made impressions of both their own hands and feet, recording them for posterity!

The molds, after drying, are painted with watercolors. On the third or fourth day after painting, children seal in the colors by brushing shellac over the molds. After permitting molds to dry for several days, they are taken home.

Another popular class project is building bird feeders. There are several places to find the simple bird feeder building plans. The first place is usually the high school wood shop. The media center is another good source. Finally, when all else fails, a parent may offer assistance. A tie-in with the bird feeders is a class project finding the proper food for feeding.

We found many birds love bread and cookie crumbs. The blue jays, tree sparrows, juncos, grackles, robins, and cardinals are especially fond of bread and cookie crumbs. A favorite of chickadees, tree sparrows, juncos, brown creepers, and woodpeckers is peanut butter mixed with cornmeal smeared on a bark or into cones. Blue jays like to eat whole corn.

Fruit eaters, mockingbirds, catbirds, thrushes, robins, and blue jays love apples, bananas, raisins, cherries, oranges, and grapes.

Some birds prefer chicken feed, corn, and fine ground eaters. These include certain sparrows (tree, song, fox, and white-throated), goldfinches, cardinals, chickadees, and nut hatchers.

Nearly all birds love ground-like hamburger. Sunflower seeds are eaten by most birds.. These would include crossbills, grosbeaks, and purple finches. If your school cafeteria has any leftovers such as mashed potatoes, the blue jays and starlings will have a feast! Their menu also includes left-over cottage cheese, baked potato skins, cheese, and sausage.

If the beginning teacher needs assistance, the local Audubon Society will certainly assist. They have always been an excellent source for this teacher.

Several years ago, this teacher was asked to write a course of study for an outdoor education summer school program. Though the task was involved, the material gathered was extremely useful in science classroom instruction. The course of study encompassed in-depth experiments that included soil, plants, water, and animal life.

SOIL

Children were asked to look for the color, texture, structure, depth, and reaction to pH (the checking of acidity or alkalinity). We measured the thickness of the duff layer, topsoil, subsoil, parent material, and identified the bedrock, if present. Charts were made to record the five areas listed. With the reaction to pH we had a graph line chart going from most acid (0), to slightly acid (6.5) to neutral (7) to most alkali (14). We also recorded the temperature of the layers, whenever possible. The work was summarized with a list of plants, insects, and animals that one finds on the surface and within the top four inches of soil in a particular field study area. These have included spiders, worms, ants, snails, fungus, and molds. If time permits, the teacher could also study or measure the slope of a field study area and determine the best use of the land. An area or sheet for kinds of erosion was also used. Some questions asked by our children included, "Was the erosion sheet rill, gully, bank, or splash?" "What was the evidence?" "How much soil was lost?" "Great or small?" We also included, in this study, a glossary of words ranging from accelerated erosion to a water table.

SOIL

Chart #1

THICKNESS OF:

TOPSOIL
SUBSOIL
PARENT
BED-DUFF LAYER
MATERIAL ROCK

COLOR:

TEXTURE:

STRUCTURE

DEPTH

REACTION TO pH

TEMPERATURE

SOIL

Chart #2

SOIL REACTION TO pH

Most Alkali *

(14.0)

Neutral
- **(7.0)**

Slightly acid
* **(6.7)**

Most Acid*
 (0)

PLANTS

Plants grow at different levels in the plant community. We have the upper level, middle level, and lower level. Children are asked to collect, identify, and classify trees, shrubs, bushes, flowering plants, ferns, mosses, grasses, lichens, fungus, and molds. Included are charts that identify the different parts of plants. The unit on plants also includes a glossary ranging from acrid to volva. If time permits, the beginning teacher may want to do an in depth study of trees. This would include finding the ages of trees, measuring the diameter of trees, finding the height of a tree without climbing to the top with a tape measure, and finally estimating the board foot volume of a tree.

Most children are fascinated by the importance of rotten logs to the living community. The late, Dr. Anne Dunham was an exceptional teacher who has had a lifelong affect on this teacher's experience on the nature trail. She informed my students that rotten logs of fallen trees provide homes and food for animals and a place where certain plants can grow. When the log decays into soil, it changes the texture, color, depth, water-holding abilities, and richness of that soil.

WATER

The study begins with a sample of a running stream. Children work with a chart listing the headwaters of a particular stream near our school. Is the slope of the stream bed steep, fast, flowing? Are the rocks large, small or sand? Is the water temperature very cold, moderate, or warm? Is the amount of usable oxygen for fish a lot, enough, or variable? What kind of insects have you found? Hayfly, stonefly, bellgrammite, caddis fly, Mayfly, beetles, worms, bugs, spiders, midge, or larvae? Questions asked were, "What effect of temperature is there on water life?" "Do we find life at temperatures greater than seventy-five degrees Fahrenheit?" "How about from sixty-five to seventy-five degrees?" "From forty to sixty-five degrees?" "Is there any life below forty degrees?" "What is the effect of pH on water life?" By using the same chart as previously given, where do we find the greatest amount of life? List the plants and fish. For those children who are looking for a challenge or desire to be extended, ask them to find the cubic feet of water, per second, in that stream. (We multiply the average width times the average depth times the number of feet per second and that equals the cubic feet of water flowing per second.)

A handy device is to hand your children a Xerox copy listing how to calculate one cubic foot of water. This is water in a container measuring one foot wide, one foot high, and one foot long. A water flow of one cubic foot per second equals 448.83 gallons per minute. One cubic foot of water equals 7.48 gallons. It also weighs 62.4 pounds.

You may want to ask your children the following questions. "How many gallons of water flow in this stream every second? "How many gallons of water flow in this stream every minute?"

The teacher is aware that the stream flow in cubic feet per second times the gallons in one cubic foot of water equals the number of gallons of water per second. The other question, we multiply gallons per second times seconds in a minute and that equals the number of gallons of water per minute.

WATER

Chart #1

WATER TEMPERATURE

Do We Find Life At?
- **Temperatures greater than 75 degrees Fahrenheit?**
- **Temperatures between 65 to 75 degrees F?**
- **Temperatures between 40 to 65 degrees F?**
Temperatures below 40 degrees F?

DOES pH EFFECT WATER LIFE?

WHAT TEMPERATURE HAS THE GREATEST AMOUNT OF LIFE?

LIST ALL THE PLANTS AND FISH IN THE FOUR CATEGORIES :

1st Category
2nd Category
3rd Category
4th Category

(75 degrees)
(65-75 degrees)
(40-65 degrees)
(below 40 degrees)

WATER

Chart #2

CUBIC FEET OF WATER IN A STREAM

Have you ever gone fishing and wondered how much water was flowing by you every second? Every minute? Every hour?

To find the cubic feet of water per second, in a stream:

Multiply the average width of the stream, times the average depth of the stream, times the number of feet of water flowing per second.

EXAMPLE:

1 Cubic Foot of Water = 1 foot wide of water by 1 foot high of water by 1 foot long of water.

A water flow of one cubic foot per second = 448.83 gallons per minute.

1 Cubic foot of water = 7.48 Gallons
1 Cubic foot of water = 62.4 pounds

ANIMAL LIFE

This area is broken down into two large groups. The first is **invertebrates,** having no backbones. The second is the **vertebrates** who have backbones.

Charts are given to name, give the size and description, food preferences, and value. Some questions you may ask are, "How does wildlife affect the soil, water, plants, other wildlife, and man?" "What changes has man made in the environment which may cause these animals to move to other areas?" "Can you suggest anything which might be done to improve the habitat?"

Children are asked to identify and label all body parts of the insect. A carry-over from making plaster molds, is having the children cast animal tracks. They are taught how to clean the track, very carefully, of loose particles of soil, twigs, and any other matter. Then we spray the track with shellac from a pressurized can. The children form a two-inch wide strip of cardboard or tin into a ring surrounding the track. They press firmly or ask the teacher to help them press the cardboard into the ground to give support. We allow at least one inch to form an edge of mold for plaster. Children carefully mix two cups of plaster of Paris in a tin can adding water slowly until it is as thick as heavy cream. We carefully pour the mixture into the mold until the plaster is about to top. In about fifteen minutes we carefully lift it out of the mold. On a wet or rainy day the hardening will take longer. We then clean the cast with a butter knife and wash it very gingerly. The children apply a thin coating of vaseline to the track and surface of the cast. We place it on a flat surface and surround the casting with a two-inch strip of cardboard or tin as before. We mix plaster of Paris and pour it into the mold, making certain that top surfaces of casting is smooth and level with the mold. If the students want to use the casting as a wall plaque, then they should place a loop of wire in back of the casting while the plaster is still soft or wet.

Sometimes I suggest an open paper clip if the casting is small. It should not be touched until the next morning. Carefully, remove the mold. The children separate the two layers and wipe excessive vaseline from the face of the cast and track. Again we scrape any rough places with the knife blade, or use fine sandpaper to smooth the rough edges. The masterpiece is washed in running water. When the cast is thoroughly dry, some children paint the inside of the track with India ink or black poster paint. Many children enjoy placing a label to name the track. A coat of clear shellac or clear plastic may be applied to protect and preserve the casting.

The course of study is contained in a booklet of fifty-six pages. The material reviewed is the essence of the work and has not included how to make an insect collection or mount butterflies, or make a micromonolith card. If your interest is outdoor education, the suggestions mentioned are intended to whet that interest.

ANIMAL LIFE

Chart #1

PLANTS AND ANIMALS FOUND ON THE SURFACE OF THE EARTH AND WITHIN THE TOP 4 INCHES OF SOIL

PLANTS & ANIMALS   YES   NO

HOW MANY?

Spiders

Worms

Ants

Snails

Fungus

Molds

Others

ANIMAL LIFE

Chart #2

INVESTIGATE & IDENTIFY

INVERTEBRATES   (NoBackbones)

VERTEBRATES   (Backbones)

Name of your Invertebrate:

Name of your Vertebrates:

Size of your Invertebrate:

Size of your Vertebrate:

Description:

Description:

Food Preference:

Value:

Food Preference:

Value:

WALL MURALS

One summer several years ago, a very talented artist, Nicholas Cappiello, painted colorful figures on the walls of buildings of my day camp buildings in Ringwood, New Jersey. The first thing the artist did was tape-measure the space on the walls where the pictures would be painted.   He returned two weeks later.

When he returned, the artist taped a large brown paper on the wall.   Large pin holes outlined a large, happy bear drinking milk with a straw. My very good friend then took out a sock containing crushed charcoal and evenly tapped the sock against the many pin holes. This has been the technique of many past artists including Michelangelo painting the Sistine Chapel.   When Mr. Cappiello removed the brown paper from the wall there was a black dotted outline of the bear. The artist then traced the outline dots with paint and filled in the shadowing and figure with paint.

In the course of the school year, children brought in white sheets of paper and outlined figures. We supplied several nylon panty-hose containers of crushed charcoal. The children made the pinholes on their pictures. Following the same procedure as Nicholas Cappiello, they transferred the picture to a white paper, covered classroom walls.   The children used colored magic markers to brighten up the figures and added sprinkles to make some of them sparkle. We decorated the classroom walls and a hall bulletin board.

The novice teacher should be aware of ideas found everywhere. Develop the ability to see the correlation of tie-in possibilities of everyday experiences with classroom activities.

JUNE

Poetry, Reading, Grouping, Experience Folders, Permanent Records

LAST MONTH

With the completion of the year's classroom work, some teachers may have some extra time before the last day of school. When this is my situation, I return to the language arts textbook that briefly delved into poetry. Our school media center has several audio tapes of poetry that is used to spark children's interest.

POETRY

Some children like poetry. If poetry is something you would like to develop, it would be a good idea to begin to create your own set of reference material. There are many directions one may go and many techniques used to teach, as well as styles. What this teacher does is to give each child a sheet of six main thoughts.

It begins with some clues used in writing poetry, such as, two or three syllable words. With those words, the accent is usually on the first syllable. If suffixes and prefixes have been added to a word, the root word is usually accented. In words ending in "tion" and "sion" the syllable before this ending is usually accented. A shift in the primary of a word may change the meaning of the word. In words of two or more syllables, one syllable is stressed more than the other(s). Finally, when there is only one vowel letter in a word, it usually has the short sound unless it is at the end. When two vowels are together, usually the first is long and the second is silent.

Give examples of the major kinds of poetry. The small letters denote the unstressed sound. A capital letter means a stressed or hard sound.

Children receive a copy listed above as well as the following guidelines. **IAMBIC** has a de Dumm sound. Words like ba LLOON, deLIGHT, en DURE, ma CHINE.

TROCHAIC has a DUMM de sound. Words like MO ther, STEER ing, ROCK er.

ANAPEST has a de de DUMM sound. Words like un de SERVED, re pre SENT,

In com PLETE.

DACTYLIC has a DUMM de de sound. Words like MER ri ly, GA ei ty, TEL e gram, and VI o let.

SPONDAIC has two masculine syllables that include hum drum, heart break, house boat.

PYRRHIC contains two feminine syllables such as rough season, of storms.

The children are told that a line of one foot is called a monometer. Two feet is a dimeter, then we have trimeter, tetrameter, pentameter, hexameter, heptameter, and a line of eight feet is called an octometer.

The beginning teacher may want to write an example on the chalkboard.

Ba LLOON/	ba LLOON/	ba LLOON	ba LLOON	ba LLOON
1 foot	**2 feet**	**3 feet**	**4 feet**	**5 feet**

This line of poetry is called **IAMBIC PENTAMETER**

The novice teacher may want the class to listen to tapes of poetry geared to their grade level and reading ability. In reading, this teacher tries to select some work familiar to all the children. Try to stress syllables of each word.

HICK o ry, DICK o ry, DOCK; or HUMP ty DUMP ty SAT on the WALL.

The beginning teacher may want to write a poem on the chalkboard such as:

Whose WOODS/ these ARE/ I THINK/ I KNOW

de DUMM   de DUMM de DUMM de DUMM

Ask your children, "What is the line of poetry called?" A little girl, Mary Mayonnaise responds, "Iambic Tetrameter!"

You smile at Mary and nod, "Excellent, Mary, you are absolutely correct!" When we listened to A.E. Housman's "To An Athlete Dying Young," we identified it as Iambic Tetrameter. When the class wanted action, we read Alfred Lord Tennyson's, "The Charge of the Light Brigade." Be sure to stress the words with the reading. CAN non to RIGHT of them; CAN non to LEFT of them. You may ask, "Well, class? Jot down what you think it is on a sheet of paper." After a few minutes, challenge the class. If someone answers dactylic dimeter, give them a "high 5."

The next challenge I love to give my class is Edgar Allan Poe's, "Raven." It is a classic example of trochaic octameter. ONCE up ON a MID night DR eary, WHILE i PON dered WEAK and WEA ry.

It can be fun for the novice teacher. Two children had fun with Joyce Kilmer's "Trees" and William Wordsworth's "I Wandered Lonely As a Cloud." By stressing the accents the teacher helps children become aware of structure.

After several weeks of chalkboard work and simple classroom assignments, try to have children create their own pen. A great deal of latitude is allowed, especially the first week. Children are permitted to borrow lines from one another or work in small groups of two or three. Later, they take pride in creating something all their own. Teachers often have a parent or aide type all of the children's poems into a booklet and distribute them to everyone in class.

READING

In the more structured aspects of helping our children to read, a beginning teacher may have some difficulty knowing where to begin. Though many schools have reading specialists to help a child in need, the classroom teacher should be able to be aware of reversals and inversions, that is, children substituting words for those they have difficulty with, omissions, repetitions, failure to try to pronounce a word, insertions, and word-by-word reading. Many teachers know the best way to improve reading is to read at whatever reading level the child is capable of reading. We also know there is no, one best reading program. This teacher has always been successful with phonics and sounding out words. Be sure your program is adapted to the needs of the students and the available facilities and personnel.

To help us with our children we should know the child's intelligence quotient, the child's mental age, the education of the parents, the occupation of the parents, the medical record of both children and parents, and finally, the emotional problems of the children and their parents. These and many other factors are related to learning how to read and to the differences in reading ability which will inevitably emerge in any first grade class.

A school's "master teachers" having ten years of outstanding experience, and hopefully, past the child bearing stage of her life should be teaching first and second grades. They should receive a carte blanche ticket for any books or materials wanted. Classes should be no more than fifteen children.

If a child has a poor learning experience at the lower primary grade levels, the gaps of learning becomes greater. The need of additional remedial teachers increases. More importantly, we know success breeds success and failure feeds on failure.

The novice teacher should be aware of the importance of perusing children's previous standardized reading scores. This will aid in streamlining an individualized lesson plan for the present class. In kindergarten, many school districts use the Metropolitan Readiness Tests. They measure word meaning, sentences, information, matching, and the child draws a man. The scores include reading readiness status and a percentile.

The first graders usually receive the Stanford Achievement Test, Form J. This test evaluates paragraph meaning, word meaning, and spelling.

The second graders take the same test as the first graders, except the form is K.

In the third grade children usually take the California Achievement Test, Form W. This test measures reading vocabulary (word recognition, meaning of opposites), comprehension, reference skills, interpretation of material, test of word form, capitalization, punctuation, word usage, and spelling.

Some tests that will be useful to the beginning teacher wanting to improve the reading skills of their class includes the Dolch Oral Reading Test and the Gates-MacGinitie Reading Tests.

The Dolch is noted for testing sight words in isolation and will sometimes reveal a child knows more words in actual reading than he does in the sight recognition of words in isolation. Often a child miscalls small words in sustained reading situations he may be able to correct immediately. This indicates he has not mastered small words.

The Gates is noted especially for its method of obtaining scores in comprehension and vocabulary. It is especially effective in the first three grades.

One other test may be note mentioning. It is the Gray Oral Reading Test. The emphasis identifies such errors made in mispronunciation, words not attempted, omissions, substitutions, and repetitions. This becomes evident when the child reads orally. Each paragraph is timed. Scoring involves recording the number of errors, types of errors, time elapsed in reading each paragraph, and a comprehension score. The total score can be converted into a grade-equivalent score.

GROUPING

My favorite grouping plan is called the Modified Joplin Plan. Under this plan, for example, six teachers divide a large group of children. The children are divided according to the grade level of their ability in each core curriculum subject.

It should be common knowledge of differences of readers within the same reading level. By homogeneous grouping, what we do is to narrow down the differences thereby making the task of each teacher much easier and more efficient. Experience with the Modified Joplin Plan has witnessed my group of children advancing an average of three years in approximately seven months of teaching.

Principals and other administrators shy away from the Modified Joplin Plan primarily because of parental pressures. Some parents want their children in the same class as the "kid across the street." To avoid confrontation, most administrators favor the heterogeneous plan of having all levels or several levels of reading ability children in the same reading class. This potpourri of abilities is an injustice to all the children since they all read at different levels. If a teacher teaches reading for sixty minutes, every child should receive an equal portion of teaching time, every day. This is not possible. In forty-one years of teaching I have never seen or heard of a successful heterogeneous reading, math, science, language arts, spelling, or social studies class that has extended all children to their limits.

The Modified Joplin Plan should begin at the third grade level and continue through high school. An ideal situation would be for all reading teachers to have such supplemental materials as the EDL controlled reader and the junior tacistoscope. They should also have ready access to the Xerox machine and computer master material as well as any other materials suggested by a veteran staff. The prime time for reading each day is the first thing each morning. The most effective amount of time for "scheduled reading," is one hour each day.

Experience indicates children should have an explicit study of phonics, learning the alphabet, learning the sound of each vowel and consonant and the importance of syllables. All these are indispensable building blocks of our language. Any child, unless brain damaged, can be taught to read.

HOMESTRETCH

June, usually begins with band members leaving class to go to the primary schools and giving them a recital. To me, this is tragic for both the band members and the primary grade children. Lost class time can never be replaced. Perhaps your school has a Freedom Day honoring either the missing soldiers, astronauts, or a new president. It is also the time for the School's Awards Assembly. At this time Field Day awards are distributed. Academic Achievement and Perfect Attendance Awards are also distributed.

Both teachers and children feel the onrush of the summer vacation. Perhaps your principal will also get into the act by unloading tons of forms, notices, and whatever into your mailbox. He states he would like the forms completed and into the office, "yesterday." Two very important tasks teachers are required to do is checking out the experience folders and completing the permanent records.

EXPERIENCE FOLDERS

Most probably you will have your class experience folders in your classroom filing cabinet. They are usually arranged alphabetically, according to a child's last name. Some teachers study them at both the beginning and end of the school year. Many teachers are instructed to remove any and all material that is outdated and insignificant. That would include last year's attendance card, old pieces of art, old report cards, last year's workbook supplements, and previous year's notes from parents. What should remain in the folder includes, recent standardized test results, Child Study Team referrals, this year's duplicate report card, and anything else requested by your principal.

PERMANENT RECORDS

The permanent records are most often stored in the school office filing cabinets and locked. It is the teacher's responsibility to update the permanent records by recording the child's final grades in all subjects. The teacher is also responsible to record the child's attendance and whether the child was promoted or retained. In forty-one years, I have never seen or heard of a child being retained.

There is another section of about five lines where the teacher is asked to comment about that particular child. At one time only teachers and other school personnel had access to the permanent records. Today, parents may ask to see their child's record. It is their legal right. Most comments are made or at least should be made and recorded with some thought and sensitivity. It is not unusual to find misspelled words and incomplete sentences. Finally, it is the responsibility of the classroom teacher to be sure to glue both the child's latest picture and the results of the California Test of Basic Skills scores in the permanent record.

A week before the last day of school, each child should clean out their desk and hall locker. It is not unusual for a student to find a forgotten lunch bag dating back to September or October. Some still have winter gear and other miscellaneous belongings. Textbooks are usually collected the day before closing. The last day of school is most often ended at noontime with class parties beginning at about eleven o'clock. A class mother and her assistants bring in the soda and other goodies. She leaves and about ten minutes before noon the final report cards are distributed with the future class lists read.

The last day is one of relief and sadness. The year was exhausting with daily challenges and demanding deadlines. As the children look appreciatively at you as they leave, perhaps you'll pat each on the head and whisper, "May God bless each and every one of you always. I've given all of you my best shot."

INDEX

Leaving class 13-4, 115
Legend of Sleepy Hollow 58
Lesson plans 39-40, 64-5, 90

March 63-72
Marionette play 27, 88-9
Master teacher 18, 47, 49, 112
Mathematics 4
May 90-107
Media Center 15, 18, 28, 74, 80, 88, 91, 108
Michelangelo 15, 107
Modified Joplin Plan 114-5
Mozart, Wolfgang Amadeus 15
Murals 107
Music 25-8, 38, 57, 60

National Education Association 71
National Merit Scholarship 64
NBC Building 56
New Jersey 17-8, 53, 55, 63-4, 67, 70
New Jersey Assessment Tests 63
New Jersey Education Association 19-20
Newton, Sir Isaac 15
New York 54-6, 70
New York Post 71
New York Times 54-5
Nonsensical frivolities 38-40, 59, 66
November 17-30

Objectives 32-4
October 11-6

Additional copies - Ship to: (Please print)

Name:
Address:
City, State, Zip:
____copies of book @ $14.99
Postage & handling @ $3.99 per book
Check for total amount enclosed.
Make checks payable to:
PRIOR PRESS OF LAKEWOOD
P.O. BOX 546
LAKEWOOD, N.J. 08701

Also published: "EDUCATIONAL INEPTITUDE:
       A NATIONAL CRISIS"

Awaiting publication:
"HOW TO ORGANIZE, ADMINISTER, AND
SUPERVISE A WORKSHOP FOR GIFTED &
TALENTED CHILDREN"
"THE MARTYR" (a biographical novel of
Girolamo Savonarola)
"COMPANION WANTED" (a category romance
novel)

About the author*

Francis Filardo has taught all subjects at the elmentary level for twenty-one years. He also has twenty years of teaching math, science, history, physical education and directing a program for the gifted and talented at the secondary level.

The author was a New Jersey guest speaker at the U.S. Health, Education, and Welfare conference in New York City. The New Jersey Commissioner of Education selected the author as its spokesperson at the education symposium held at Princeton University. He has been a guest lecturer at several graduate universities. The author was a New Jersey Education Association member of the Committee for Exceptional Children, for three years in Trenton, New Jersey. Mr. Filardo is an honorably discharged Korean War veteran.

The author received two summer educational sabbatical leaves spanning six years. The summers were spent studying the educational systems in Europe. He was born and raised in East Harlem, New York City and received a full, four year scholarship to Seton Hall University, South Orange, New Jersey. Mr. Filardo has a B.S., M.A., and an extensive graduate research and study portfolio.

PRIOR PRESS OF LAKEWOOD, INC.
P.O. BOX 54, LAKEWOOD, N.J. 08701